SUCCESS
IN
MARRIAGE

Success in Marriage

DAVID R. MACE

ABINGDON PRESS   NASHVILLE • NEW YORK

SUCCESS IN MARRIAGE

Copyright © 1958 by Abingdon Press

ISBN 0-687-40554-8

Library of Congress Catalog Card Number: 58-9521

MANUFACTURED BY THE PARTHENON PRESS AT
NASHVILLE, TENNESSEE, UNITED STATES OF AMERICA

PREFACE

As a marriage counselor, I have listened to people's stories of marital difficulties, and tried to resolve them, in all of the five continents—in Europe, Asia, Africa, Australasia, and America. In all of these continents I have worked to develop new marriage counseling services and to improve services that were already in existence. I can therefore confidently claim to know something of the needs of men and women in their efforts to make of marriage the rich and satisfying experience it ought to be. I know also something of how these needs can best be met.

In this book I have tried to put down in simple and readable form some of the fruits of my own thinking and experience in this field. Here are the people I have had in mind as I was writing:

First, I hope there may be value in the book for young people looking toward marriage. The best way to cope with marriage problems is not to allow them to develop at all! It is easier to do this if the possible dangers are known in advance. So I hope some young lovers will read the book, and I hope they will find it helpful.

Second, I am thinking of the average married couple, jogging along happily enough, with no serious problems. It is a sad mistake to imagine that, because a marriage is not in bad trouble, it is as good as it could possibly be. Many husbands and wives, I believe, make the mistake of expecting too much early in marriage, and then of expecting too little later on. I have tried in this book to encourage ordinary married couples to widen their horizons and to see hitherto unrealized possibilities in their relationships. There are too many mediocre marriages in our midst.

Third, I have had in mind very often the married couples who are in trouble—the discouraged and bewildered people whose dreams are not coming true. For twenty years I have worked to help such people, and I know well the anguish and distress they suffer. Out of my experience as a marriage counselor I have tried to talk about some of the difficulties which couples have so often talked over with me. My hope is that this may be a book which a kind friend can put in the hands of a couple in difficulties and which will help to show them the way out of their troubles.

Twenty years ago I became convinced that there was no more needy work than to help men and women toward success in marriage, for on this so much of their own happiness and of the community's welfare depends. The intervening years have been full and busy ones, for there is much to do in this field. Nothing that has happened during those years has altered my original conviction. It remains as strong today as it was at the beginning. It is out of that conviction that I have written this book.

DAVID R. MACE

CONTENTS

Part Four—*Five Perplexing Problems*

Part One

Five Basic Principles

CHAPTER I

CHOOSING

Dr. Van de Velde, the Dutch gynecologist who devoted so much of his life to helping husbands and wives find happiness, spoke of the ideal marriage as a temple resting on four cornerstones. The first of these, he declared, was the choice of a suitable partner.

This is inescapably the starting point for anyone who wishes to marry. "How *can* he marry," the old nursery rhyme querulously demands concerning Little Tommy Tucker, "without e'er a wife?" No one will question the inexorable logic of this simple statement.

It is not, however, just a partner—any partner—that is wanted. No doubt if men and women were paired off for life by having their names drawn out of a hat, some successful marriages would result. But we cherish the conviction that careful selection, on the basis of matching qualities, would yield decidedly better results. Insofar as we have as yet investigated this question scientifically, the results support our conviction. Well-matched couples seem to have much better chances of success in marriage than the ill-assorted.

So as young people come to maturity in our Western world, they must, if they have a mind to marry, face the task of finding a suitable partner. Most of them give this choice a good deal of careful thought and even suffer a good deal of anxiety over it. And well they may, because upon this choice much of their future happiness depends.

The choice was not always theirs to make. And it would not

be theirs even now if they had been born in some other part of the world. Today in the East the majority of marriages are still arranged by the parents. Sometimes the young people are scarcely consulted at all. A Chinese student of mine told me that her parents didn't meet until their wedding day. They were introduced and then immediately married. In some communities there weren't even any preliminary introductions! The bridegroom was allowed to lift the veil, and look for the first time at his bride's face, after the wedding ceremony was over!

I once asked a group of young Indians if they wouldn't rather choose their own marriage partners as we do in the West. To my surprise they said "No." When I asked why, they said because they were too inexperienced to choose wisely. They preferred to leave it to their parents.

An Indian girl followed this up by asking a question. "Is it true," she asked, "that in the West a girl has to make herself attractive to men in order to be sure of getting a husband?" It was a new angle, but I had to admit that it *was* true.

"Well," she responded, "I'm glad I don't live in the West. We Indian girls don't have to worry. We *know* we'll get a husband. It will all be arranged for us by our parents."

But we live in the West—and therefore we have to do our own choosing. Maybe we prefer it that way. But even if we do, it represents a big responsibility for a person still young and with limited experience of life—to choose the person you will live with, in the closest and most intimate of all adult human relationships, for perhaps the next fifty years. Clearly a choice of such magnitude should be wisely made.

How *do* people choose their marriage partners? The Greeks

had a pretty legend about how in the beginning men and women were joined together in pairs. Then, in capricious mood, the gods playfully tore them apart and shuffled them like a pack of cards. After that they had to search until they rediscovered each other. Your true mate was your lost opposite half.

Many people still cherish the idea of the soul mate—the Mr. Right who will one day, like Prince Charming, walk into the lovelorn maiden's life and imperiously claim her as his own. We imply this when we say of two people that they were "made for each other."

The scientific facts unfortunately give little encouragement to such pleasing fancies. Researches in mate selection reveal that the factor which determines choice in the overwhelming majority of cases is—propinquity!

The reason why most couples marry is that they are thrown together by circumstances, discover that they have interests and needs in common, and so find themselves attracted to each other.

Selection on this basis can obviously be largely a matter of blind chance, and less intelligent than the choices made by conscientious parents in the East—who, to do them justice, often search widely and are not easily satisfied.

There is in fact no doubt that some of our young people make foolish choices of their marriage partners. We can hardly blame them for this. How can they do any better if they are given little or no help? Since we parents no longer do the choosing for our sons and daughters, surely the least we *can* do is to give these young people some standards to work on. Yet often this is not done. And young people, lacking guidance in terms of reason, fall back on the only natural guide they have—emotion!

"I *know* the boy I'm going out with is the right one for me," said a seventeen-year-old girl to me once.

"What makes you so sure?" I asked her.

"Because," she replied, "whenever I meet him, I tremble all over like jelly!"

No doubt it was an achievement for the boy to induce such emotion in the girl, and no doubt the girl found these emotions pleasurable. But really, what does shaking like jelly have to do with the suitability of these two persons to enter together into a lifelong relationship and the founding of a family?

Alas, very little. Yet in the absence of any rational basis for action, do we not all follow the promptings of our emotions and act, as we say, instinctively?

Can we offer young people something better? American psychologists have tried to produce scientific tests of compatibility. To get the green light the man and woman must achieve a minimum total of positive points between them or their graphs must stay near enough together on the squared paper.

When I relate this to my English friends, for some reason it makes them laugh contemptuously. In principle I have nothing against such tests. They may seem a bit cold-blooded. But heaven knows, marriage is a serious proposition. It is a lifetime undertaking—not a dream in the moonlight. And if I had reason to believe that any test would increase the chances of success for any couple, I would vote for it with both hands.

However, all that the tests really find out is whether the couple have enough maturity and enough in common in the areas where community of interest is known to be crucial, to have a fair chance of success. I believe that the average couple, who intend to take marriage seriously, will be likely to find

16

this out anyway in the course of a normal courtship and engagement. The couple who *don't* take marriage seriously would never dream of taking tests anyway!

What then can we say that will help young people to choose as wisely as possible? There *are* some established facts, based on wide experience and supported by research, that can be offered. Let me list them.

1. *Maturity* in those concerned is important. I mean, chiefly, emotional maturity. To avoid complications let me define this very simply as the stage at which you have grown enough to have a reasonably good knowledge of and acceptance of yourself and a capacity to understand and get along smoothly with most other people. A few exceptional boys and girls reach this point relatively early in life. In general, however, I think it is unusual for a girl under twenty, or for a boy under twenty-two, to be mature enough to marry without taking unwarrantable risks. Most people who marry too young do so because they are maladjusted personalities trying to escape from their conflicts.

2. *Length of acquaintance* comes next. We have all heard of the couple who met on a summer holiday, fell madly in love, married in a few weeks, and lived happily ever after. We are less likely to hear of the other couples who followed the same course and ended in disaster. Marrying in a hurry is a game of chance. It is gambling with the life happiness not only of the two concerned but also of children yet unborn. In all too many cases, alas, the reason for the haste is that one of these latter is already on the way!

Other things being equal, two people are more likely to see each other in proper perspective during a lengthy acquaintance than during a brief one. The first illusions are gradually shed, the pretenses and deceptions fall away, the realities emerge and are clearly apprehended. American researches have found that marriages based on a close acquaintance of a couple of years or so proved to be decidedly more stable than those in which the couple knew each other only a few months before they became man and wife.

3. *Values shared in common* seem to matter a good deal in wise choosing. Marriage between people of quite different backgrounds have been known to turn out very happily. But in general the evidence suggests that all wide disparities—of age, of race, of religion, of culture—introduce hazards into the proposed union which must be taken seriously. Where such hazards exist, other factors should be overwhelmingly favorable in order to restore the balance.

These hazards cannot always be clearly perceived before marriage. People who are "different" are often epecially attractive to us on that account. Unhappily there is a sharp contrast between this relatively superficial attractiveness and the tensions which may arise when the two people concerned come together in the deeply shared life of marriage.

For successful marriage two people need not, however, be alike in all respects. Variety of tastes, and in some degree even of temperament, offers scope for a marriage which may enlarge the horizons of both partners. What is basic is that both should feel and think alike about the standards, values, and principles upon which their philosophy of life is based, and should have the same fundamental attitudes and outlook.

Much more could be said about the choosing of the marriage partner. Yet I believe that these are the principles that matter most. The couple who have reached reasonably mature judgment, have come to know each other well, and find that increasing knowledge of each other tends to deepen their sense of unity and their respect for each other as persons—this couple may with a reasonable measure of confidence go forward into marriage on the assumption that they have what it takes to build a sound and satisfying relationship.

CHAPTER II

PREPARING

When John and Mary are together, the sense of ecstasy they experience eclipses all else. They are in love. They are going to get married. They are overwhelmingly happy. What else matters?

But when each is alone and thinking of the future, who knows what unspoken questions echo in the secluded corridors of their minds?

"Shall we always be happy, as we are now?—How can we make sure that this delight and sweetness that is ours will last on through the years, will stand the test of time?—Why do some marriages that seem to start so well end in failure?—Is there anything we can do to make our future happiness secure?"

There are several ways of trying to answer questions of this kind. One would be to visit a fortuneteller, who would gaze dreamily into her crystal ball and pry open the closed book that holds the secrets of the future. Another would be to visit a marriage counselor and to undertake a program of careful preparation for marriage.

Naturally, I am heavily biased in favor of the second alternative! And not without reason. Of all the means that lie within our power to influence marriages in the direction of success or failure, adequate preparation beforehand is in my opinion the one likely at present to prove most effective.

One of the peculiarities of our society is the fact that often more efforts seems to be expended on the preparation for the wedding than on the preparation for the marriage. A wedding is admittedly a highly significant event in the lives of those concerned, and no effort should be spared to make it memorable. But a wedding is, after all, no more than the beginning of a marriage, as a birth is the beginning of a life. A wedding is all over in a single day. A marriage may last for half a century.

The way in which two people spend the period before their marriage can influence quite definitely what happens in the marriage itself. Indeed, the courtship and engagement period is, so far as the unfolding of the relationship is concerned, continuous with the married life of the couple. They are moving progressively, all the time, toward deeper intimacy and fuller commitment. Marriage is simply the point in their growing together at which they declare formally and publicly that they are ready to enter the deepest intimacy and the fullest commitment.

The wedding ceremony is indeed a beautiful and solemn event. But it is an illusion to imagine that a ceremony in which two people participate necessarily adds anything to, or changes anything in, the lives or personalities of those people. They are essentially the same people in the week following the wedding day as they were in the week preceding it.

This may seem to be making light of the religious ceremony and of the divine blessing that is solemnly invoked. That is not my intention. I believe that two people with religious convictions will have sought the blessing of God long before they take their final vows at the altar; indeed, the ceremony is really the outward manifestation of their inward experience. On the contrary, no invocation will make much difference to two people without religious convictions, because they will not

21

create the conditions which would make the blessing effective.

How then ought two people looking toward marriage to prepare themselves, so as to give themselves the greatest possible chance of lasting happiness? Let me list first what they can do by themselves, then discuss what they can do with the help of others.

1. They should *learn all they can about what marriage means.* A great deal of study has been devoted to the marriage relationship in recent years, and as a result we have accumulated new knowledge that can be helpful to any couple. This knowledge is now available in books.

If you were planning a long journey into unfamiliar country, you would want to find out beforehand as much as you could about the conditions of life there. You would do this in order to avoid making needless mistakes and to make your trip as pleasant as possible.

Marriage is a great venture into a new kind of experience. Yet plenty of couples get married without reading a single book on the subject. They will study books on cookery, books on car management, books on gardening; but it never occurs to them that there is anything to learn concerning the great art of marriage!

The fact that you are reading this means, presumably, that if you are unmarried you agree with me! At the end of this book I have listed some titles for your further reading.

2. They should *get to know each other really well.* I have stressed this in the chapter on choosing. The question I want to answer now is "How?"

Two married people once told me about something they did during their engagement. Throughout a whole summer they went for one evening each week to a pleasant, peaceful spot on top of a hill which commanded a beautiful view. Here they took turns telling each other their whole life stories. No detail was considered too trivial. Finally, they reached the point at which there was nothing more to tell, because they knew everything about each other.

That seems to me to be a very sensible plan. Some things, of course, are not easily told. If in doubt, it's a good idea to tell them first to some trusted neutral person. Whether *everything* should be told in all cases is a matter of opinion. My own view is that it is best to do this if possible. The most satisfying kind of love is based on complete knowledge, complete understanding, and complete acceptance of each other.

3. They should *use the experience of courtship to grow in their relationship*. Engaged couples make a mistake, in my view, if they confine their activities to enjoyable and effortless undertakings. People who meet only in their best clothes, on pleasure bent, don't develop the deepest kind of friendship. It is in working together, in surmounting obstacles, in enduring stress, that teamwork is truly tested. And marriage must be teamwork, or it is doomed.

Marriage involves an extended and complex process of interpersonal adjustment. A certain amount of this adjustment can and should be made before the wedding day, enough at least to give the couple confidence in their capacity to resolve conflict and grow together, for without this their chances of lasting happiness are poor.

In short, the more adjusting they can do to each other now, the less there will be to do later. Married life inevitably brings a whole series of new situations of its own to which husband and wife must accommodate themselves.

It is foolish for couples to prejudice their chances of success by carrying over too many uncompleted assignments from the engagement period and piling them on top of the formidable array of new tasks with which married life itself will confront them.

4. They should *plan the future together*. This doesn't mean that they have to make hard and fast decisions about every detail. But they should aim to reach agreement in principle about all basic questions—where they will live, whether the wife will work, how they will budget their money, what will be their policy toward friends, neighbors, and relations, what children they want and how they will bring them up, and so forth.

I am sometimes amazed to find married couples who never troubled before marriage to discuss the way they would live together when they became husband and wife. I have had to deal with wives who complained bitterly that their husbands gave them no money, yet admitted that they had never raised the subject before they married; and wives who discovered after marriage, to their consternation, that the men they had married disliked children and had no intention of having any! These are extreme cases, but I hope they make the point.

By this time I may seem to have turned the courtship and engagement period into hard work! I don't believe that is true. On the contrary, I think couples who do these creative, constructive things together will get more real satisfaction out of their growing relationship than those who spend all their time holding hands in the moonlight.

However, I'm not finished yet. There are further ways of

preparing for marriage that need the help and co-operation of other people. Let me refer to them briefly.

An excellent idea is to join one of the marriage preparation discussion groups that are being organized by churches and social service agencies in many parts of the country. This is a relatively new idea, but it is proving very popular. Almost any couple will benefit from serious discussion about the meaning of marriage with other engaged or recently married couples.

If you have any fears, misgivings, or uncertainties about marriage, let me beg you to go and talk them over with a marriage counselor. You will find the counselor sympathetic and understanding, and everything will be in complete confidence. To carry unresolved anxieties into marriage is a most unwise policy, which may lead to unhappy results for yourself and for the one you love.

It is a good plan to consider having a medical check-up before marriage. Married people take each other for what they are, and it could prevent unhappiness later if they exchanged health certificates at this important point in their lives. This may be conveniently combined with the taking out of an adequate insurance policy on the life of the young man. Also, any difficulties or uncertainties about the physical side of sex can be cleared up during this visit to the doctor.

· Finally, if your marriage is to be a religious ceremony, its meaning will be greatly enriched for you if you seek together to understand its full implications. Quite possibly the minister, priest, or rabbi will in any case arrange to go over the service with you beforehand. If not, I'm sure he would be delighted to do so at your request.

In recent years the idea of preparation for marriage has

gained wide acceptance. This is all to the good. In field after field of human endeavor we have sooner or later to accept the simple rule that the best progress can be made only by understanding clearly what we are doing, by being equipped with sound knowledge, by preparing ourselves in advance and following a well-formulated plan. To blunder blindly into any great and complex undertaking is increasingly recognized as folly and irresponsibility.

If we can choose for ourselves, for our children, for our friends, between going into marriage prepared for it or unprepared for it, can there be any possible doubt about what we ought to choose?

CHAPTER III

ADJUSTING

A successful marriage normally passes through three stages. First comes the short but blissful period when the emphasis is on *mutual enjoyment.* This is what the honeymoon ideally ought to be—a time when the sheer ecstatic joy of belonging to each other puts a song in the hearts of bride and bridegroom. All honeymoons, alas, don't turn out like this. As a general rule, the better the couple are prepared for marriage the more likely they are to have a successful honeymoon.

But in the nature of the case, the honeymoon can't go on forever. It isn't practicable to live in a state of ecstasy. It would in fact be quite dangerous in any modern city! So there is the coming down to earth again, the return to work and responsibility, the taking up of the routines of married living.

This need not be in any sense dull or even disillusioning. Even if it were, disillusionment is after all just dis-illusionment—the shedding of illusions. The fewer the illusions the couple have brought into marriage, the better!

As the married couple settle down after the honeymoon, a second stage begins—a period in which the emphasis is now on *mutual adjustment.*

Successful marriage is essentially the achievement by two people of a complex process of adaptation to each other in a close and intimate relationship. As we have seen, no two people can expect to be tailor-made for each other in advance. So some adjustment will be inevitable. The amount of adjusting which will be necessary will vary from one marriage to the next and will depend generally on two factors.

First, it will depend on how much the couple are alike and how strong their personalities are. Colorless people with little assertiveness and few aspirations may need to do very little adjusting in order to jog along together in a mediocre marriage. Those who have strong wills of their own may, on the other hand, have a lot of work to do to bring these wills into reasonable harmony. Once this has been achieved, however, the marriage may prove to be a very happy one for both.

The other factor is how much people are expecting from their relationship. In some societies marriage is considered to be little more than a superficial exchange of mutual services on the basis of I'll-scratch-your-back-if-you'll-scratch-mine. The man thinks of his wife as a source of sexual relief and a way of having a place where he can get a good night's sleep and three meals a day at reasonable cost. The wife thinks of her man as someone who will give her security and enable her to fulfill her womanhood by having children. Beyond that not much is expected.

Today, however, the tendency is to look for much greater depth of relationship in marriage. Love, comfort, understanding, companionship, tenderness, affection—these are the words we use again and again. But we often fail to realize that the closer people come to each other in this kind of relationship, the greater the tensions that can be aroused, and therefore the more complex the adjustments that may have to be made. This is one reason why so many married couples are in trouble today—because they are expecting so much more without realizing that this steps up the price!

When the necessary adjustments have been successfully made, the marriage passes into the third stage, in which the emphasis is on *mutual fulfillment*. This is a quieter and less exacting state of bliss than the ecstasies of the honeymoon. Yet in many ways it is more satisfying, because it goes deeper and is much more enduring.

The critical stage for the success of a marriage, clearly, is the adjustment period. All marriages inevitably involve the partners in the need to make *some adaptation* to each other. Anyone who goes into marriage without a willingness to submit to change is cheating. The man who expects to remain exactly the same person, doing exactly the same things after his marriage as he did before, just hasn't grasped the significance of what he has undertaken. Marrying a wife is not merely adding a useful and ornamental appendage to your personality. It is entering upon a radically new and different way of life.

This business of adjusting is so important that the whole of the next section of the book will be devoted to some of the major adjustments that the married couple will have to make. At this point, let us focus attention on the adjustment process itself.

Just because married life is so close and intimate, husband and wife are bound to disagree at times. No two people are always of one mind about everything. Disagreement produces conflict. There is a clash of opposing wills and a struggle for supremacy. Each tries to defend his or her own way of thinking against the other. The result usually is a quarrel—a fight in which the weapons are words and emotions.

To a devoted couple who have been all lovey-dovey this is a painful crisis. But let's be sensible about it. Conflict is quite natural and quite inevitable in marriage. Indeed, it is healthy, because it reveals where an adjustment has to be made; and if the conflict is used constructively to make the adjustment, the marriage is strengthened as a result.

Let me stress this. To avoid quarrels in marriage is not necessarily virtuous. Sometimes one partner will give in for the sake of peace. But if a principle is at stake, that is a foolish policy. "Peace at any price" no more improves family relations than it does international relations.

Another way to avoid quarrels is to bury the conflict. "Let's agree never to raise the subject again." This solves nothing. It means an agreement that there *can* be no agreement. In marriage that is a crushing defeat. It means accepting an area of permanent estrangement. Some couples may have to settle for that. But in doing so, they settle for a second-rate relationship.

So some amount of quarreling is normal in the adjustment period of marriage—and even occasionally later. Of course, couples quarrel in different ways and with varying intensity. Some people hate arguments of any kind; others seem almost to enjoy them. Within acceptable limits I believe it is good for husband and wives to be exposed to the full heat of each other's emotions—both positive and negative. Barbara says, "It was only when Tom got so worked up about my lateness that I realized how important punctuality was to him." Tom responds, "And it was only when Barbara broke down and howled about that concert that I saw clearly that taking my wife out once a week was for her not a luxury but a necessity." Emotional intensity is often the only way we have of underlining the statements we make. In quarrels we communicate something important to each other—something that isn't easily communicated in any other way.

However, what married people quarrel about isn't always the real issue. Frank was deeply hurt and resentful because Alice had proved to be sexually unresponsive. A basic adjustment in their marriage wasn't being made. The result was that every time Alice crossed him, even in a trifling matter, Frank tended to blow up. So when he stormed at her for disarranging the papers on his desk, that wasn't the real reason for his hurt feelings. When two married people quarrel violently about something unimportant, it usually means that they are using the immediate issue as a battlefield to work off deeper hostilities.

So what matters in marital adjustment is not whether or not husband and wife quarrel, but whether they understand why they quarrel and know what to do about it. A quarrel always means something quite specific—that hostility has been aroused and has sought an outlet. Hostility is like electricity. It is generated by friction. It is potentially dangerous. But it can be put to work if properly channeled.

Some people consider it wrong to feel angry. It is in fact quite natural to do so. Anger is a state of discontent with things as they are. This can of course be quite useless. If you merely beat your fists against a door because it is locked, you use up energy to no purpose. And if you merely rage and storm because your marriage is disappointing you, the likelihood is that you will only create further cause for disappointment. But if your anger leads you to take steps to provide yourself with a key to open the locked door, or to work for better adjustment in your marriage, you are making progress. Indeed, a great deal of human progress has been made in just that way.

Suppose Frank and Alice, after they have argued fiercely about the arrangement of his desk, were to sit down and ask themselves and each other just what went wrong. Alice might say, "But, Frank, you surely didn't get worked up like that just because of the desk, did you? Are you angry with me because of something else?" Frank might sit quiet for a minute and then reply, "Yes." It would then be for Alice tactfully to find out what Frank's problem was. Then all the facts would be out in the open. Alice, being a wise girl, would realize that Frank's sexual frustration was bad for him and bad for the marriage. But she would then have to admit that she didn't know just why she was unresponsive, but that it was so, and that she seemed unable to help it. They would now have used the quarrel to get at the real issue. From that point they would have a chance, with help if necessary, to face this difficult adjustment and so remove a potential threat to their marriage.

Of course all adjustment in marriage doesn't involve conflict, and conflict doesn't necessarily always show itself in quarrels. But I have dwelt on the question of handling quarrels because it is at this point that married people so often get into difficulties. Perhaps we can try to sum up.

1. All marriages involve adjustment, and often the more you expect of marriage, the more adjustment is needed.

2. Adjustment is made necessary by the fact of disagreement and conflict, which are quite normal in such a close relationship.

3. Conflict often reveals itself in quarrels between the married couple. In itself, quarreling can be quite helpful if it reveals the deeper feelings of husband and wife to each other.

4. However, quarrels need to be analyzed afterwards to see why they happened. As long as couples know just why they quarreled, they can and should make the necessary adjustment so that they needn't repeat that quarrel.

5. If they *don't* know why they quarreled, because the conflict lies too deep, they should seek the help of a marriage counselor without undue delay.

CHAPTER IV

SHARING

Speaking in India to a Hindu group, I was trying to explain marriage counseling.

"Tell me," I asked, "what happens in a Hindu home when husband and wife disagree?"

"That never happens," was the answer.

This was baffling.

"Why not?" I challenged.

"Because," they explained, "from early childhood the little Hindu girl is brought up to believe that her husband will be to her as a god. And when she marries, it is so. He can do nothing wrong, say nothing wrong, in her eyes. So they never disagree."

That is one way to ensure peace in the home. This is patriarchal authority in full operation. In such a marriage all the adjustments are made by the wife.

For a considerable part of human history in most parts of the world, marriage has been more or less like that. The subjection of women to men, inside and outside the home, has been taken for granted. Relying first on his superior physical strength, then on his exclusive possession of economic power, the man has held the position of dominance. The wife's position has been subject. In some societies her husband held the power of life and death over her.

This is not just a matter of ancient history, either. Before the passing of the Married Women's Property Act in England in 1882, a wife owned nothing in her own right. On marriage, all she had previously possessed became the legal property of her husband. And his power over her did not stop there. Provided he did not resort to extreme violence, he was entitled to use corporal punishment in bringing her to a properly subservient frame of mind.

In those days there was no doubt about who was boss in marriage. However, it would be wrong to infer, as some have done, that in consequence all husbands were tyrannical. Often they didn't in fact use the powers accorded to them. Even when they did, all wives didn't knuckle under meekly. Women are resourceful, and through long centuries of subjection they have learned to achieve their ends despite the overwhelming odds marshaled against them. A wife has a thousand ways of making life miserable for her husband, and the average husband has always known it and treated her with due respect. However, if the contest between them was pushed to the last extreme, there was never any doubt as to who had the whip hand.

Then, in the early 1890's, at the other end of the world, a startling thing happened. New Zealand gave women the vote, declaring them to be politically equal to men. Once started, there was no stopping this movement. Within the lifetime of the older women among us, one of the greatest revolutions in human history has swept across the world. Today only a few countries remain in which women may not vote. No one knows how much longer these countries will continue to hold out.

The result has been that woman's status in the modern world has undergone a radical change. She has climbed to greater and greater heights of political, economic, and social freedom, until now she is almost completely recognized, in Western society at least, as the equal of the man. Even this does not represent the limit. In America a book has appeared entitled *The Natural*

Superiority of Women. It was written, significantly enough, by a man! The wheel has turned full cycle!

This revolution in the status of woman outside the home could not leave her position as wife unchanged. The towering figure of the husband has been progressively scaled down to a size commensurate with that of the woman at his side. In some cases the process has gone even further. "The modern husband," said an American sociologist, "has lost status heavily. Once he was an august figure. Today he's a sap and a dope."

But this is going further than the woman wishes. The emancipated girl of today wants a "fifty-fifty marriage." "We go into this as equals, John and I," she declares. "Share and share alike. That's the way I want it."

What have these tremendous changes really done to marriage? Can we try to assess the new situation?

The word "equal" has confusing implications when it is applied to men and women in the marriage relationship. So long as we are thinking of their co-operative undertaking as two persons who have gone into partnership, it is valid enough. Someone has said that marriage is two-party government, and in that sense, equal voting powers look like plain justice.

Yet in the little kingdom of the home I think it has usually been the queen who ruled. A recent Australian study of the seat of power in modern urban marriages, seeking to discover which partner makes most of the important decisions, reveals that on these terms the wife is unquestionably the boss. But was it really so very different before? Of course the husband *thought* he made most of the decisions. Doubtless he *announced* them. But did he really *make* most of them, alone and unaided? I wonder.

What, then, have wives gained today? More power, certainly.

Yet perhaps not as much more as the modern girl is inclined to think.

And what have wives lost? A good deal of security in marriage, without any doubt. As an authority figure the husband of today is a pale shadow of his former self. Accepting his devaluation, he has scaled down his sense of responsibility to match. He does not feel the ancient obligation to stand by his wife and children. He isn't the tent pole any more, and the show can therefore go on if he walks out of it. In disturbing numbers this is just what many modern husbands are doing.

The quest for equality, in fact, is a false quest. It applies mechanical concepts to human relationships, which is always bad practice. The person who is loudly demanding equality is all too often really jockeying for position and won't be satisfied with equality when he gets it.

If having a boss in marriage is undesirable, having two rival bosses is even less desirable. This is not really what the modern wife wants, even if she thinks it is what she wants.

The really exciting possibility in marriage today is that it needn't have a boss at all. It can be a flexible relationship in which all decisions are arrived at by mutual discussion and agreement.

This sounds simple—but it isn't. You simply can't develop that kind of relationship unless you have two people who know each other very well and trust each other completely. They must be people who are pretty mature, too. And they must be ready to take their marriage seriously enough to give time to working it out.

Given these conditions, however, great possibilities emerge. Psychological studies show this syncratic co-operative pattern, as it is technically called, to be far and away the best for stable and happy marriages.

The achievement of this bossless pattern in marriage rests on two fundamental principles—the resolution of the couple to reach a common mind in all situations where they encounter a difference of opinion, and their willingness to delegate authority to each other according to which one is really the more competent in the area in question.

Reaching a common mind on any issue can be very time consuming, yet once this process has been really accepted as a working method, its vast superiority to all other methods becomes plain. Through it the couple gain increasingly deep knowledge of themselves and of each other as persons. This knowledge clears the way for easier decisions in the future. It becomes possible for husband or wife in the midst of a discussion to smile, admit an unsound motive, and yield ground. How much better than battling on stubbornly in defense of a case you know is already lost, just because you mustn't lose face!

The syncratic method is cumulative in its effectiveness too. "Each victory will help you some other to win," as the old hymn says. The time and effort needed to reach a common mind become greatly reduced. As in a court of law, previous decisions render future ones easier to make.

Can a marriage then really work without a boss? Well, not entirely. What the "fifty-fifty" principle of today really makes possible is a continuous transfer of authority back and forth between the couple. Like a team of racing drivers, both take turns at the wheel. And they try to share the duties in terms of proved competence. "Here, John, you take over. You're better at this kind of thing than I am."

There are susceptibilities, however, that must be respected. The wife who knows she is a better driver than her husband won't endanger his male prestige among his friends by taking the wheel when they are out together with the crowd. The husband who has a magic touch with refractory children won't give a public exhibition of his skill in a situation that would discredit his wife as a mother. Each will recognize the need to build up the other's status in the social circle in which they move.

The roles of both men and women are changing a great deal in the modern world. The husband as boss has been dethroned. This may be interpreted by the modern wife as a great victory. But what does she want to do with her victory?

If she ascends the throne in his stead, she will gain nothing that can have any value for her. I suggest that the arguments about who's boss will get us nowhere at all. What we want, and what we can have if we're ready to work for it, is the marriage in which leadership is responsibly shared. And that is best of all.

CHAPTER V

MATURING

A marriage is a relationship, and a relationship is a living thing. It must, as we have seen, be fostered and sustained.

But that of itself is not enough. Because it is living, a marriage must grow. It is dynamic, not static. It must move—either upward toward maturity, or downward toward degeneration. One thing is certain—it will not stand still.

Growth in a relationship can be measured in many ways. Maturity could be regarded as the point where conflict is entirely absent and the couple are of one mind. It could be measured in terms of their deep, continuing happiness together. I am inclined to feel, however, that both peace and joy in marriage are not ends that can be attained merely by actively seeking them. They are not so much goals as manifestations of the fact that the true goal of marriage has been reached. And that goal is creativeness.

An exhibition in Germany once organized a competition for the nearest approximation to a perpetual motion machine, the prize to go to the entry that kept running longest. A visitor who arrived found that all the competitors' machines had stopped except one. He examined it, fascinated by the smooth, effortless movement.

"This is wonderful!" he exclaimed to the inventor. "Wonderful! Tell me, what does this machine *do?*"

"Do?" cried the inventor contemptuously. "It doesn't do anything! It just keeps going! Isn't that enough?"

For a marriage that is definitely not enough. Just as life must have direction and purpose, so must a relationship. Two people deeply in love, caught in the rapture of a moment of supreme ecstasy, often wish that time would stand still. But time will not stand still. It moves on, and the spell is broken.

Love that is to be enduring must have a creative purpose. Love of its very nature is creative. Its maturity is not an empty-handed detachment from life, but fruitfulness in the midst of life.

So a marriage must have some worthy end which it exists to serve. "Two people wrapped up in each other," said some-one, "make a very small parcel." Indeed, it is worse than that. Two people who live for each other exclusively will not generate love. They will, ultimately, generate boredom and restless dis-satisfaction.

Two young lovers may be accurately portrayed as standing facing each other, their hands joined, and gazing lovingly into each other's eyes. But you can't go on indefinitely gazing into someone else's eyes. You are liable to develop a squint! Anyway, there are other matters that call for attention. So the portrayal of mature lovers would see them side by side, looking together toward the goal they have set themselves, and not standing still but eagerly striding forward. The love that endures must be active, creative, and purposeful.

J. D. Unwin, the sociologist, held the view that a marriage could not reach its fullest maturity unless the partners shared an allegiance to some purpose outside themselves which they considered to be ultimately more important even than them-selves or their relationship. This is carrying the idea of the creativeness of love a stage further, in that the goal for which the couple strive is not just a means of bringing their love to maturity. It is not merely a means to an end. It is an end in it-self—an end of such importance that they will if necessary sacrifice even their own happiness for its attainment. We are here, quite clearly, in the realm of what we call "spiritual values."

The obvious way in which this works in a normal marriage is that the couple find their common sense of purpose focused in the care of their children. The joy of parenthood is the beginning of love's creativeness for many a couple. In toiling together to provide the best they can for the new life they have together brought into being, they experience the maturing of their love. This is something deeper and more enduring than the moonlight thrills of their courtship days. As their eyes meet across the cot in which lies their sleeping child, John and Mary know the strength of a love that has been braced by a shared purpose. Something else, something other than themselves, now takes first place in their lives; and they realize it not as foreboding, but as fulfillment.

However, parenthood is not of itself the means by which love matures. It would be truer to say that parenthood tests searchingly whether married love is becoming truly creative. In some marriages parenthood is seen, by one partner or the other, as an obstacle in the path of pleasure, or at best as a duty to be discharged. Even those who wholeheartedly welcome the coming of children may do so for motives that are far from mature. They may see their children as adding something to themselves—prestige, security, ego satisfactions—so that they are objects of desire rather than objects of love.

Children, in fact, cannot fully meet the need for purpose that marriage must have in order to grow to maturity. Children come and go. The marriage needs of itself a sense of direction that is there before the children come and that will endure after they go. This guarantees to the children the freedom to be themselves. It is dangerous for married couples to invest so much of the creativeness of their love in their children that life loses its meaning when the children disappoint them or leave them. True parental love should be unpossessive and undemanding. The best parents are those who, loving their children dearly, yet sometimes speak eagerly to each other of the day when the children will be off their hands and they can give more time and energy to the other things in life that they care about. It is good for parents and children alike that there should be these "other things." Mature married love does not find its expression first and foremost, or exclusively, in the parental task.

What husband and wife need for the full maturing of their relationship is a sense of shared destiny, a feeling that they are members of a team working in a great cause, united in the service of mankind. Some of the most deeply happy married couples I have known have found their happiness in pursuing together the destiny which they deeply believed they had come to share.

For people of deep religious faith this need in marriage is ideally met. Such couples see their love as partaking of, and reflecting back, the love of God. They see their union as ordained within the unfolding of a divine purpose which embraces them and all mankind. They see their goal as being to unite in serving their fellow men in whatever way they feel God has called them to serve. Their happiness is deep and enduring precisely because they never make happiness their first objective. For one of life's strange but inexorable paradoxes is that "the pursuit of happiness" is a self-defeating activity. The deep contentment that we all desire comes not when we set out resolutely to enjoy ourselves, but when we lose ourselves in some creative task, some self-forgetting service.

42

Rev. C. Wayne Perry, Pastor

In a marriage that grows to full maturity the creativeness of love builds the lives of husband and wife into a unity that is expressed physically, mentally, emotionally, and spiritually. Through their sense of shared destiny they find not only that their hearts are in tune with each other, but that they are in tune also with the rich and varied life of the world about them. This is well expressed by Felix Adler. Speaking of the married couple whose love has grown through the years to its full maturity, he says:

Together they have traveled the road of life, and remembrance now holds them close, remembrance of many hours of ineffable felicity, of a sense of union as near to bliss as mortal hearts can realize, of high aspirations pursued in common, of sorrows shared— sacramental sorrows. And now, nearing the end, hand in hand, they look forth upon the wide universe, and the love which they found in themselves and still find there to the last, becomes to them a pledge of the vaster love that moves *beyond* the stars and suns.[1]

[1] *Incompatibility in Marriage* (New York: D. Appleton and Company, 1930), p. 15.

Part Two

Five
Major Adjustments

CHAPTER VI

SEX

There are good reasons for starting our detailed discussion of marriage adjustments with sex. This is the first major adjustment that most newly married couples have to face. Unless they make reasonable progress here in the early months of marriage, their adjustment in other areas of their relationship may be affected. Moreover, in this area the marriage counselor again and again finds problems that are the result of ignorance and misunderstanding.

Sexual harmony in marriage is of considerable importance to the happiness of the couple. Serious frustration and hurt feelings related to sex are very disturbing to both husband and wife and can very soon destroy their feelings of warmth and tenderness toward each other. This is much more clearly recognized today than it was in the Victorian era, when sex was considered to be a subject unfit for public discussion.

However, now that we can discuss sex freely, we must avoid going to the opposite extreme and imagining that if married people can only learn the right "technique" in intercourse, everything else in their relationship will be perfect. That is very far from the truth. I have known several couples who early in their married life achieved a sex relationship which was exactly right by the standards of the sex manuals, but that didn't prevent the marriages in question from ending in disaster.

What this means is that the sexual side of marriage is closely linked with the emotional and personal elements in the relationship. To put it in technical terms, the sex relation is a function of the total response relation, which is emotionally and not physically motivated. Sex, at its fully human level, is the servant of love, the means by which love is expressed.

What the married couple have to achieve, therefore, is a sex relationship that expresses, sustains, and renews their deepest and most tender feelings for each other. If they fail to do this, they will sooner or later lose interest in each other sexually. As an unhappy wife once put it to me, "We don't have intercourse any more. You see, there's nothing left for it to express."

It would take a whole book to cover adequately all that is involved in sex adjustment in marriage. Such books are available and are included in the section "For Further Reading" at the end of this one. All I wish to do in this one chapter is to summarize what I consider to be the important points.

The young couple should of course have some knowledge of the anatomy and physiology of the sex organs. In my opinion, however, many books about sex adjustment in marriage tend to go into unnecessary detail about this. It is the mental and emotional attitudes that matter supremely. If the right emotions are absent, sexual functioning becomes physically impossible; and when sexual functioning breaks down, it is rare that it can be traced to physical causes alone.

I am going to assume a knowledge of the basic facts about sexual intercourse, omit the usual little anatomy lesson, and consider instead how husband and wife *feel* about sex. Their feelings are similar in some ways and different in others.

The basic feelings are alike. There is first a longing for bodily closeness, bringing mutual stimulation which produces an anticipatory sense of exhilaration. This leads to an increasing and exciting tension which Havelock Ellis called tumescence. As the bodies of husband and wife become more and more responsive to each other in the rhythmic movements in which their desire is expressed, the tension mounts higher and higher till it reaches a peak of ecstatic feeling which is usually followed by sudden explosive release. At this supreme moment of breathless excitement there is a momentary loss of consciousness which the French call *"le petit mort"*—the little death.

The explosive release of tension is called the orgasm or climax. It is followed by a satisfying experience of general relaxation and a pervading sense of deep contentment and peace. This dying away of excitement and the return to emotional normality is called detumescence.

So far, the feelings of husband and wife are very similar. Now for the differences.

The basic role of the husband in the sex relationship is an active one. He is the initiator. The wife's role is to respond. At least, this is true in general. It doesn't of course mean that the wife plays an entirely passive part. She may take the initiative at a number of points. But even when she is doing so, her real object is to encourage initiative in her husband. Essentially she is the person acted upon, the one who responds. Unless there is active desire in her husband, there is nothing for her to respond to, and she cannot fulfill her feminine function.

Again, the whole experience is simpler and more direct for the man. He simply obeys an intense drive toward a clear goal. Because his is the active role, he makes the movements that build up and satisfy his own desire. For the woman, feelings are more complex and more widely diffused. The atmosphere and setting of the love-making may affect profoundly her capacity to be sexually aroused. She must contrive to fall in step with her husband's movements and tune them to her mood so that they stir and satisfy her desire along with his.

Often, too, the reactions of the wife are slower than those

of the husband. The Kinsey research suggests that this is not always so, and not necessarily so. But whatever the cause, it does in fact happen in many instances. The wife takes longer to be ready for sexual union; consequently the husband may have to extend the preliminary love play till she is thoroughly aroused. She takes longer to reach the climax, so that the husband may have to control his mounting excitement and slow down his movements till she can reach the summit either with him or before him. She needs a longer, slower process of relaxation after the climax has been reached, and she will feel hurt if her husband turns away and falls asleep too soon. He should stay with her till for both of them the sensations have completely died away.

If the couple starts with a clear picture of this pattern of emotional responses, they can then experiment together until they have learned how to use their bodies to bring to both of them the most satisfying experience possible. The question of what position they adopt in intercourse, for example, is of secondary importance. There is no "correct" or "proper" way to "perform" sexual union. There is only one goal—to find the best means by which the particular couple can, as an expression of their mutual love, meet and satisfy their sexual needs in and through one another. If they do this, there will be no dangerous frustrations to tempt them to turn away from each other in quest of the fulfillment which they have failed to find in their marriage.

Attaining this goal takes time and may require a good deal of experimentation. The experiments the couple make together won't always succeed. They should be ready for this and take it all in the right spirit, not allowing themselves to be hurt or offended, and laughing at themselves sometimes. They will need to be free to talk about their feelings and responses, too, and to tell each other what they find most satisfying. In the end this should lead to a delightful understanding and openness between them in which they accept their own and each other's sexual needs as natural and right and good, and are as eager to give satisfaction to each other as they are to attain it for themselves.

Married couples should judge their use of each other's bodies in terms of the result they achieve in giving each other relief, comfort, and delight. If they strengthen, deepen, and intensify their feeling of attachment to each other, they are using sex as it should be used. If they alienate and offend and frustrate each other, they are misusing it.

What is true of the positions they adopt is also true of the frequency with which they have sexual union. There is no yardstick. Variations in frequency are so great from couple to couple, and in the same couple at different periods of their married life, that it would be foolish to make rules. Each couple must find out what their needs are and do their best to satisfy those needs, avoiding the tensions due to frustration on the one hand and the lack of zest that comes from excess on the other.

Married couples often find that their individual needs don't correspond. In fact, it is unreasonable to expect that any two married people would always want to have sexual intercourse at precisely the same times and with precisely the same frequency. Where there is real love and understanding, this difficulty can almost always be met, because each is eager to make the other happy. There is always some way of giving relief to a needy partner, and no truly loving husband or wife would demand more than the other is able to give. In this spirit of give and take, I believe practically all problems of so-called "sexual incompatibility" can be resolved. Sex, I repeat, is the servant of love. If the emotional attitudes between husband and wife are right, the couple's adjustment to each other at the physical level of sex usually follows naturally.

The opposite, of course, is true. If, despite every effort, husband and wife cannot achieve a mutually satisfactory sex adjustment, it is almost certain that something is wrong with the emotional attitude of one or both of them. They need the help of a marriage counselor.

Most modern couples, in their sex adjustment, have to take into consideration the possibility of pregnancy which is nearly always present. The principle of family planning is today practically universally accepted, in the sense that no group of people believes that it is the bounden duty of the married couple to have the maximum number of children which they are biologically capable of producing.

There is disagreement, however, as to the methods that can be used to avoid conception taking place. To Roman Catholics certain methods are forbidden by their church, and it is only right that they should loyally honor the standard they are required to accept, and take their problems to counselors of their own faith.

For most others the only consideration is to find the method which will prove most reliable for the couple concerned. The best guidance on this subject can be obtained from the Planned Parenthood Federation, the address of which may be found in the back of this book.

CHAPTER VII

MONEY

"You can sum up the cause of most marriage problems," said a probation officer with long years of experience of domestic wrangles in court, "under three headings—sex, in-laws, and money. And, if you ask me, I'd say money was the most common cause of all."

It is probably true that married couples quarrel as much about money as they do about anything—especially if their financial resources are limited enough to require skillful handling to avoid going into the red. In this chapter let us examine the relationship between money and marriage.

First, we must realize that great changes have taken place in the course of the past century. Until 1882 a married woman in England technically had no money at all except by the indulgence of her husband. And for long years after this disgraceful state of affairs was legally adjusted, the husband retained the habit of holding tightly to the purse strings and doling out to his wife whatever he thought fit.

Indeed, the idea that the family finances are exclusively the husband's province still lingers on rather generally. Working-class wives have admitted to me that they don't know how much their husbands earn; attempts to find out only move the men concerned to righteous indignation. And still today, in all income groups, I meet wives who say that they almost have to go on their bended knees to implore their husbands to buy them new clothes.

These are, however, relics of a dying era. Today, as we have seen, the vogue is the "fifty-fifty marriage." The economic emancipation of women has made marriage a financial partnership. Everywhere the number of working wives is on the increase. In the modern two-income home, sometimes it is the wife who takes home the bigger pay check. In America young husbands work for university degrees while their wives assume the function of the breadwinner. The students bestow upon these devoted wives the mock degree of P.H.T.—"Putting Hubby Through"!

This new system is obviously more democratic than the old. Injustice is avoided when each has an equal say in the way the family income is spent. But this also opens the door to far more quarreling than in the past. It may have been unfair for the husband to thump the table with his fist and roar "No" in response to his importuning wife. But at least it settled the matter, and no more was said.

Nowadays a great deal more has to be said. There's no short cut to the working out of a sound policy of family spending. It takes literally hours and hours of discussion. And often the discussion touches on very tender spots. It's hard to give up that coveted new hat and put the money into savings instead!

In fact, it gets harder than ever in an age when more and more of our goods are priced not by their total cost but by the down payment. It used to be considered disgraceful, if not positively sinful, to run into debt. But that's all out of date. The new pattern began with the mortgage on your house. If you haven't a chance of buying a home outright for twenty years, it seems sensible enough to close with an offer that lets you live in it during those years and pay as you go along. Then the same principle worked down to smaller items and shorter periods, until today it is an accepted pattern to be almost continuously in debt. "If we put off paying the rent this month, and don't license the car, we'll be able to make a down payment on a refrigerator," says the wife in the cartoon hopefully to her husband!

But this kind of thing, carried too far, is disastrous to the peace and concord of the home. One of our problems today is that getting married usually means a drop in living standards for the young people concerned. "Remember that tupenny buns are fourpence when you get married," a friend warned me when he heard of my engagement. The young husband and wife, if they are looking ahead to home owning and parenthood, have to make sharp cuts in the luxuries to which in the care-free single state they became accustomed. This is a test of their love. It isn't pleasant to fumble in your pocket for the usual coin and find it's no longer there. If marriage hasn't brought solid and satisfying compensations, you can soon begin to persuade yourself that you've made a bad bargain. Then the trouble starts. Money quarrels are a sure sign that the partnership of marriage has broken down, that you've gone back to thinking in terms of "I" and "you" instead of "we."

Let me try, out of my experience of dealing with marriage problems, to lay down some basic principles for the management of family finances.

1. *All the facts about relevant financial matters should be fully known by both partners*. This means that the wife has a right to know just what her husband earns. The man who says, "This money is mine. I worked for it and I earned it," is implying that his wife is a sleeping partner in the family concern. Maybe if he could stay at home for a few days, cook the meals and clean the house and wash and iron and take care of the children, his perspective would be duly corrected.

It means, too, that there should be no secret nest eggs hidden away, no undisclosed debts incurred. These are the symbols of distrust. If you can't put all the financial cards on the table, it means that your marriage isn't based on the full mutual trust that leads to the deepest happiness.

2. *All the available money should be regarded as belonging not to one partner or the other, but to the family as a whole.* This doesn't necessarily mean that everything has to be lumped into a joint bank account and check books served out to all the family members. A check book can be a dangerous weapon in some people's hands. Distribution of the financial resources is a wise principle accepted by all thoughtful investors. But there should be an understanding that, if a great enough need should arise, any money earmarked for one purpose can be automatically switched to serve another end.

This is where wives sometimes hold back. They seal off private hoards they brought into the marriage or expect to be maintained by their husbands and to use their own earnings for personal spending. In essence this is a vote of no confidence in the husband, and he knows it and is hurt by it, even if he never says so.

3. *The policy to be adopted in using the money should be agreed on after mutual discussion, and agreements reached should be strictly honored on both sides.* If there is more than enough income to cover the needs of the couple, an uncontrolled joint account will no doubt work. But to those who have not attained this blessed state of affairs, some sort of budget must be drawn up if trouble is to be avoided. It doesn't really matter who keeps the record. What matters is that the couple should know how much they can spend in each area—rent, food, heat, light, insurance, clothes, holidays, and so on—and so keep the money situation under control.

Budgets are best drawn up on a weekly or monthly basis and for a year at a time, because the emphasis shifts from season to season. You have to work at first on an experimental plan. It's not wise at any time to be too rigid about family finances. The aim is not to frame unalterable laws but to plan frequent consultations. By all means, when the occasion really demands it, buy or give beyond the limit set. But when you do so, decide where the cuts are to be made to restore the balance.

And always, when unauthorized expenditures are made, consult your partner beforehand, or explain immediately after. Nothing undermines confidence like the breaking of the agreement reached after careful consideration. You wouldn't spend your employer's money without approval. Treat the family finances in the same way.

4. *However little may be available, each member of the family should have a personal allowance, which can be spent freely without any questions being asked.* This is not an allowance to meet necessary expenses—the husband's bus fare or the wife's clothes. These should be budgeted. Quite apart from all that, however, I believe it is necessary to a person's self-respect that he should have money in his pocket which is completely his own, for which he is accountable to no one. To be denied this is to be denied personal liberty at a vital point.

Nothing is more demoralizing than for a wife to have to sneak a few dollars out of housekeeping to indulge in some small luxury. To a sensitive woman this can feel almost like theft. We all, however poor we are, need a little luxury now and then to give spice to life. The means to do this, freely and spontaneously, should be included in the family budget.

Incidentally, this goes for children too. As soon as a child understands the principle of spending a penny, he should have the opportunity to put it into practice. Children may never learn to manage money wisely later on if they are not provided early in life with the opportunity to learn from experience.

These are, I believe, the fundamental principles upon which the handling of money in the home should be based. Where these simple rules cannot, despite every effort, be kept, the trouble lies not in money but in some personality defect of which money troubles are only the external manifestation. The capacity to handle money with wisdom, prudence, and scrupulous honesty is a pretty searching test of maturity.

CHAPTER VIII

WORK

A marriage is a company of two formed to carry out a specific enterprise to make a home and to establish a family. This is quite a complex job, which calls for all sorts of skilled and unskilled labor—moving furniture, repairing machines, cultivating a piece of land, maintaining stocks of essential commodities, cookery, needlework, accounting, child management, and much else besides.

In the past it was often possible to employ household help to get some of this work done. Nowadays this has ceased to be practicable, and the managing directors must themselves carry out most of their own instructions. Not only so, it is necessary also that this undertaking be financed by an adequate amount of capital. Again, the two company managers are usually the only shareholders, and they must contrive together to obtain from somewhere or other the funds necessary to keep the concern afloat.

What this means, in practice, is that our marriage patterns have undergone deep changes. In the old days the man did all the work outside the home and provided the family income, while the woman did the inside work (other than heavy jobs and complex mechanical operations). Now the tendency is increasingly for both husband and wife to share between them both the inside and the outside work. Naturally this means a further set of adjustments in the modern marriage.

The idea of the working wife met heavy resistance at first, but it has now become an accepted part of our new social pattern. All over the world more and more married women are taking jobs. In Soviet Russia men and women have worked together on equal terms since the Revolution. In America the number of employed wives is now, in peacetime, greater than at the height of the war. In Britain we are told that without substantial help from married women, the labor force could not cope with the country's obligations.

But what is all this doing to marriage? How can the thousands of couples involved decide what to do for the best? What are the pros and cons in this highly controversial subject?

I'm sure there's no simple rule that can be applied to every case. It depends on the circumstances of the individual couple. And it depends on the particular point in marriage at which they have arrived.

Angela was typical of many brides of today. After a two weeks' honeymoon she and Peter took up residence in their tiny apartment. Next morning, when Peter left for his office, Angela left for hers. When they got home after the day's work, they prepared the evening meal together, tidied up the apartment, watched TV for a couple of hours, and went to bed. That became their daily routine. On week ends they did the washing, had a big cleanup, went out for an occasional evening, but otherwise rested their weary bones in preparation for the next week's work.

This was very different from Grandma's concept of getting married. But it was the way Angela and Peter planned it. Grandma's parents wouldn't have let her marry a man who hadn't enough in the bank to take care of a wife and family. But if Peter had had to meet that standard, they'd have had to wait years and years. Angela was glad she could unite her earning power with his and enable them to marry early. Their plan was to live simply, save all they could, and then start their family when they had enough financial security for Angela to give up her job.

I see nothing against this. Provided two young people are sure of each other's love, what is gained by keeping them apart on economic grounds? Being married, they can work and plan and struggle together to set up a home into which, in due course, they can bring their children. Far better spend this time in constructive and creative mutual adjustment than in futile and frustrating delay.

But there's a danger involved. Two young people can together earn a comfortable sum these days, and they can easily slip into a pleasure-toned pattern of living in which, instead of saving for the future, they gear their living to a luxury level. Then a pattern is established in which the arrival of a baby means the end of freedom and an economic nose dive for both husband and wife. That is a bad way, and a sad way, to embark on the great enterprise of marriage and the great enterprise of parenthood.

Once the baby arrives the ideal arrangement is for the wife to give up all idea of doing an outside job for several years. We are learning a great deal about human personality nowadays. Any one of the facts around which an impressive body of evidence is being assembled is that a young child's dependence on mother love is almost absolute if he is to grow into a normal, emotionally healthy adult. The impressive testimony which John Bowlby gathered from many countries and presented to the World Health Organization seems to me to be incontrovertible. The major cause of most serious personality disorder, he found, is maternal deprivation in early childhood.

Of course it isn't easy to define maternal deprivation very precisely. The absence of a mother for a few hours each day won't necessarily harm her child. There are cases where this is quite unavoidable, and I would not desire to create unnecessary anxiety. A really good mother substitute can work wonders. All the same I feel that, with all the facts before us, we ought to discourage any unduly prolonged separation of a mother from a child up to two years of age, and preferably up to four. What folly it would be if, merely to gain a few luxuries, the personality development of the child were endangered! And this undoubtedly could happen.

A wife who had three children, born at two-year intervals, would therefore face a period of nearly ten years in which motherhood ought to be a full-time job. This seems definitely to be the best arrangement, both for parents and children, when it can be achieved—and it may be worth enduring some hardships in order to achieve it.

This was the policy Tom and Florence adopted. When little Pat, their youngest, was happily settled in nursery school, however, Florence got a part-time job in a lawyer's office. This brought in enough extra money to make the budget balance despite the increasing demands of the older children. It was a long, hard day for Florence. But the fact that she was helping the family finances encouraged the children to co-operate by taking their share of the household chores. As they grew older and could assume more responsibility, the strain on the mother was progressively eased.

If children of school age were polled on the subject of working mothers, they would no doubt vote against the idea. It's nice to have an accommodating parent who is always there, ready to do whatever has to be done, as constant and dependable as the grandfather clock in the hall. But in the long run it's by no means certain that this kind of mother is necessarily the ideal. The woman who goes out to work can understand, better than one who remains in the security of the home, the experiences through which her husband and her growing children are passing. "Mother doesn't understand" is a teen-age judgment which is often more justified than we care to admit. But if Mother goes out each day to grapple with the real life of the grown-up world, she gains thereby a special kind of authority in the eyes of her children who are preparing to do the same.

Let's say that, once the children are old enough to go to school, it doesn't matter greatly whether the wife goes out to work or not. There are gains and losses either way.

In due course the children leave home. The wife's task as an active parent is over. Now she may enter a critical phase in which having a job she likes may make all the difference between fulfillment and misery.

For Mary Parrish this was a depressing time. She had been devoted to her children, and when George, her youngest, left home, the bottom fell out of her life. Fred, her husband, was busy at his job, with little time to spare. A great sense of heaviness and purposelessness descended upon Mary. She felt suddenly old and unwanted.

The phenomenal extension of the life span in recent years means that many a married woman will have a good twenty years of health and vigor left to her after her last child leaves home. For an active, intelligent woman, spending this time in cooking and housework just for the two of them may not be a sufficient goal in life. It may be a positive boon to her now to take a job, gain a feeling of social significance, and at the same time earn enough money for extra comforts, travel, or earlier retirement for her husband and herself.

How much better than moping at home, plunging into a round of superficial social activities, or degenerating into an interfering mother-in-law!

Every modern wife should feel profoundly thankful that she has today the right to economic independence. The fact that she can take a job can make life better for her at many points. She need not be driven by economic necessity into an undesirable marriage or be compelled for the same reason to endure an intolerable one. If her husband is incapacitated, or if she should find herself widowed or deserted, she can capitalize her earning power for herself and her children and save the situation.

Working wives, it seems, have come to stay. But this does not mean that all wives must work, or that any of them should work all their lives, or all their time. Taking a job can sometimes bring new strength and support to marriage and the family. But at other times it can be a threat to the well-being of either or both. It is the new responsibility of the wife of today to distinguish between these two situations and to use her new powers to strengthen the home rather than to undermine it.

CHAPTER IX

IN-LAWS

Dorothy twisted her handkerchief in her hands.

"I've just left my husband," she said. "We've been married only two years. We lived with Jim's parents. Mrs. Reynolds wouldn't leave me alone. She wants to manage everyone. I fought back, but Jim didn't support me. He gives in to her—everybody does.

"When the baby came, that was the last straw. That woman kept interfering. Everything I did was wrong in her eyes. I couldn't stand it any more. We had a big row. I finally took the baby and went back to my own parents. I've told Jim I'm not going back to him till he gets a place where we can be alone, away from our in-laws."

Dorothy's problem was typical of many that come to the marriage counselor. It is a problem I have encountered again and again all over the world. Everywhere young people are in revolt. "Outlaw the in-laws," they cry.

The widespread rebellion against in-law interference is part of a great cultural change. Actually, probably never before in human history have so few young couples lived with their in-laws. Under the old patriarchal system it was just taken for granted that, when a girl married, she and her husband would move into the home of his parents and bow to their authority. Today our new democratic ideas of the family are insisting that the young couple be free and independent, living their own lives in their own way. Since in-laws are often the greatest threat to this freedom, they become the objects of popular resentment and ridicule.

We talk of "in-laws" in general. But we must go to the core of the problem. Young husbands have been known to get into bitter conflict with their fathers-in-law. But that's a comparatively rare event. The real culprit is the mother-in-law. In a recent American study of a thousand couples with in-law problems, mothers-in-law were cited as causing as much trouble as all other in-laws put together. Also, nine out of every ten complaints about mothers-in-law came from the daughter-in-law.

This pattern is borne out by other studies and by popular opinion. The core of the in-law problem is the conflict between two women of different generations brought together by their attachment to one man. The man is at the center of the tug of war. This can be unpleasant for him. At other times he may feel flattered to have the two most important women in his life competing for his attention!

The problem tends to become most acute when the two women live together during the early years of the daughter-in-law's marriage, and especially when they have to share the same kitchen. By far the most frequent complaint against the mother-in-law is that she meddles and interferes in the young couple's affairs, and the area in which her interference is resented most fiercely is in the management of the children.

When we add up all the known facts, therefore, it is obvious that Dorothy had been in a highly vulnerable position. If in-law trouble was likely to arise in her life, she had placed herself in the most likely situation to encounter it. She had almost put her head into a noose.

All this supposes, of course, that the seeds of conflict are present. It's useless to pretend that this isn't often the case. However, it would be inaccurate to suppose that this is *neces-*

sarily so. In fact, many young couples get on splendidly with their in-laws and have no trouble at all. In the American research I have already referred to, twenty-five per cent of the couples originally approached signified that they could contribute no information to the study, because they had no trouble of any kind with in-laws! I have even known young husbands and wives who have confessed to me, with some embarrassment, that they had come to love their mothers-in-law more dearly than they loved their own mothers!

However, we are concerned with problem situations which threaten married happiness. What is it that makes mothers-in-law behave badly?

Mrs. Chanter was secretly unhappy in her marriage. Her husband was a successful businessman. Most of his life he had been preoccupied with his work. Mrs. Chanter, feeling unloved and neglected, had turned to her children for consolation. She had become a fussy, doting mother. Ethel, her daughter, had rebelled, married, and moved away. Only Arthur, her son, was left, and he was her pride and joy.

When it became clear that Arthur was serious about Iris, Mrs. Chanter was filled with panic. The prospect of life without Arthur's devotion and attention was unbearable. She did her best to belittle Iris in Arthur's eyes. Iris tried at first to be nice but soon gave up the attempt. At the wedding Mrs. Chanter was very upset. Afterwards she was fiercely critical of Iris, resented her, treated her with cold indifference. At the same time she heaped attentions upon Arthur. It wasn't that by nature she was an unpleasant person. It was just that life had become empty and purposeless for her.

Most difficult mothers-in-law are really middle-aged women unadjusted to life. They are lonely, frustrated, craving attention. Their plight is sometimes pitiful. They need, above all, warm affection and understanding. Yet by their irrational, critical behavior they cut themselves off more and more from the very things they most need. Sometimes their daughters-in-law try hard to help but are rebuffed, as Iris was.

In our day many marriages are badly upset, and some are completely broken up, by in-law tensions. Let me try, out of my experience as a marriage counselor, to make some suggestions for avoiding this kind of tragedy. How can an ideal relationship be achieved?

The foundations can be put in during the period of courtship and engagement. Young people should try to be thoughtful and considerate toward the parents of their sweethearts. When John says, "I'm marrying Mary, not her family," he has the wrong point of view. He *is* in fact marrying *into* Mary's family, and it's worth a great effort, for Mary's sake, to make himself pleasing to her parents and other relatives. In-law troubles are often based on prejudices and resentments developed before the marriage ever takes place.

On the other side, parents should try to be courteous and kind to the sweethearts their children bring home. Even if John isn't the one they would have chosen for their Mary, the choice is hers, not theirs. A critical attitude on their part won't make Mary alert to his faults. It is more likely to make her blindly defensive of him. And if she's going to marry him anyway, hostility on their part will only make things unnecessarily difficult.

Another important point for the cementing of good relationships is in the planning of the wedding. Often the boy's parents feel left out of this, and it is a wise plan to consult them and try as far as possible to meet the wishes of all the in-laws. Even if the young people have to give up some of their own pet ideas, does it really matter? On an occasion of such great happiness, surely they can be generous and make a few concessions to ensure that their families are happy too.

After the wedding great care should be taken to see that the in-laws don't feel neglected. "I don't see why I should have to write to *your* mother," says Mary. "Go and see your people if you like, but for pity's sake don't drag me along too," says John. These are unwise, inconsiderate, unkind attitudes, which are all too likely to lead to later trouble. In the business world and in our social life, we learn to be courteous and considerate toward people to whom we feel no particular natural affinity. Surely if we can do this for commercial and social advantage, we can do as much for the sake of family concord.

When difficulties arise, try to face them with patience and understanding. It's easy for Iris to say to Arthur, "That mother of yours is a nasty piece of work." On the surface, it's true. Yet underneath, Mrs. Chanter is a desperately unhappy woman. If Iris could just imagine how she feels, she could perhaps be a bit more tolerant, and the next crisis would bring less turbulence into their lives. Kindness achieves so much and costs so little.

Living with in-laws should, in my opinion, be avoided wherever possible in the early days of marriage. But where it is inevitable, experience has some guidance to give. Have a clear understanding from the start about money, the use of rooms, and mutual responsibilities. There should be respect on both sides for the privacy of the others. Separate quarters and, if possible, separate kitchens are desirable. The fact that the arrangement isn't ideal should be frankly faced, and allowances made when things go wrong. Avoid a critical, carping attitude, which destroys all harmony and peace. If serious tensions develop, an all-out effort should be made by the young couple to stand together and find a solution that will not sow seeds of bitterness in the years ahead.

Psychologically, many in-law relationships are potentially difficult to handle. Let's face that frankly. But the rewards gained by overcoming the obstacles are very great. The human spirit has a considerable capacity for adjustment, once the desirability of making that adjustment has been fully accepted. The goal to be aimed at was well expressed by the mother who said, "When Tom married Peggy, I thought I had lost a son. But what actually happened was that I gained a daughter."

CHAPTER X

PARENTHOOD

For most married couples the question of becoming parents involves a whole series of adjustments. First they have to decide whether to have a family at all. In most cases this is answered in the affirmative. Then there is the question of how many children and by what intervals they should be spaced to enable their parents to do the best for each and all. The issue of what means to use in the process of spacing them, already mentioned in an earlier chapter, arises at this point.

Then when the children come, they have to be cared for. When they are small and helpless, this means a considerable dislocation of the routines of married life. As the children grow older, however, the responsibilities of the parents do not diminish. The sheer physical toil of looking after the helpless infant is replaced by the much more complex and demanding task of guiding wisely the vigorous growth of a rapidly developing young personality. This is often a stern test of the unity and harmony of the parents' marriage.

In fact, bringing up children in the modern world can be quite a complicated business. In the old days, when obedience was the unmistakable hallmark of the Good Child, the parents' task was comparatively simple. All you had to say was, "Johnnie, don't do that!" If he persisted, you put on your most threatening voice and said, "Johnnie, if you do that again, I'll thrash you." If he still persisted, he got it—good and hard. And you went on thrashing him, without mercy, until his wayward will was subdued. So you obtained obedience. Whatever seething tumult of resentment raged within Johnnie's breast, he learned to conform outwardly to his parents' sovereign will.

Some parents today still believe this to be the right way to bring up children. Others go to the opposite extreme and take the view that if there has to be a tumult somewhere, the one place where it mustn't be is bottled up in Johnnie's breast. So they endure Johnnie's awkwardness with patient resignation. They console themselves with the knowledge that, miserable as life is, at least Johnnie isn't piling up explosive repressions to damage his personality in later life.

My guess is that most modern parents waver somewhere between those two extremes. They try being firm for a while, then repent and ease off. After a period of high-minded tolerance, however, they decide that they've stood all they can and put the screw on. All this is, of course, a little disconcerting for Johnnie. But he learns to diagnose accurately the gleam in his parent's eye and to adapt himself to the changing climate. He knows there's nothing he can do about it. "Mother's on the rampage again," he says to himself. "I'd better lie low."

But when Mother and Dad adopt different policies, there's a great deal that Johnnie can do about it. In fact, this is a heaven-sent opportunity. He learns with considerable skill to play off one against the other. Soon he is double-crossing them at every turn. There's nothing wrong with this from *his* point of view. We all have to learn to manipulate our environment to gain our own ends. This is how civilization came into being. It is the basic principle behind our scientific technology.

However, Johnnie could find plenty of other opportunities for learning how to manipulate his environment. To allow him to do it in this particular way may undermine his respect for at least one of his parents. And it may well undermine their respect for each other too. Continual disagreement about how to handle the children can play havoc with the relationship between husband and wife. Family living can become a series of skirmishes in which they are trying to score points against each other. Such a competitive spirit is a deadly destroyer of love and tenderness.

So it is important that husband and wife should reach agreement about the rules that Johnnie must learn to respect and that they will jointly administer. And it is important that in their dealings with Johnnie they should present a solid and united front. They should generally support each other even if they don't see eye to eye at the time. Then they can face their disagreements afterwards, when Johnnie has gone to bed, and adjust their future policy accordingly. If Johnnie is to become a responsible adult, he must learn to respect the law of the community to which he belongs. If he can't learn to do this in his own home, because there are no laws which everybody respects, his training for life is going to be sadly deficient.

The vital question is, *Why* do parents disagree about how to discipline their children? The simple answer, that they hold different opinions or theories, sounds convincing on the surface. But in actual fact this is seldom true. The real reason, again and again, proves to be that there is marital conflict between them, and they are using the control of the children as a battleground. It isn't really that Johnnie is playing his Mother and Dad off against each other. It is that his Mother and Dad are hitting out at each other through Johnnie.

After all, most couples have come to know each other pretty well by the time they have children old enough to present discipline problems. They have been through the courtship and engagement period and the early years of marriage. In all these experiences they should have achieved a sufficient exchange of views and opinions to know each other's minds. And where there is real love and affection, they will have had an opportunity to forge together a common philosophy of life. No two people can live harmoniously together in close intimacy of marriage unless they have agreed to accept certain common values and standards.

But surely, it will be contended, this doesn't necessarily mean that they have hammered out a plan for child rearing. The need for this will occur to many couples only when the discipline problems arise.

Again, this sounds plausible. And again, it is not true. The views we hold about the handling of our children are rooted in our fundamental attitudes of life as a whole. We identify ourselves with our children and desire for them the things we secretly aspire after. We may read books about child training and be intellectually impressed. But we will not apply what we read, in any consistent and sustained way, unless the basic principles behind the methods concerned are ones which we accept for ourselves and apply to all our relationships.

What this means is that, where husband and wife have through their mutual love arrived at a set of common convictions about life, they will work out a joint system for the upbringing of their children which is an expression of that philosophy. They will think of their relationship as a warm and satisfying experience which they want to share with their children, creating a charmed circle in which everyone loves everyone else. Dad is therefore as eager that Johnnie should love Mother as he is that Johnnie should love him, and he will carefully avoid any situation that might threaten to belittle her in her child's eyes.

74

However, when husband and wife have not achieved warm and tender affection in their relationship to each other, this entire process will be reversed. Their approach to their children will tend to reproduce all the unresolved conflicts which exist in their own relationship, just as every flaw in the lens of a projector will be reproduced upon the screen. They will find it impossible to act as a real team in their task as parents, precisely because they have failed to become a real team as marriage partners. So they will either disagree about their children, or for the sake of peace one of them (usually the father) will withdraw from the arena and hand over the whole job to the other.

Parenthood is a complex task with many facets. Nothing is more vital to its effective achievement than that it should be a co-operative task. A child needs two parents to bring him into existence. And he needs those two parents as significant figures in his world to enable him to grow smoothly to his maximum emotional development. Yet, as we have seen, he will be denied their co-operative participation in his development unless they are well adjusted to each other as marriage partners. The degree of success which they can achieve as parents is determined by the degree of success which they can achieve in marriage.

This may seem to be a startling conclusion. Yet it is one of which I am wholly convinced. I have never yet encountered a case of serious conflict between parents over the handling of their children which did not prove, after careful investigation, to be based on an unresolved conflict in the marriage. And I have found that, when the marital conflict was cleared up, the parental conflict disappeared.

Because I believe this, I take the view that parenthood is seldom of itself a cause of marital disharmony. Disagreement over the children is almost always a reflection either of marital disharmony which was already there or of tension caused by new factors which enter the marriage along with the arrival of the children. The solution of the parenthood problem lies in the solution of the marriage problem.

The supreme qualification for successful parenthood is therefore successful marriage. It is good to provide children with a nice home and nice surroundings and all the material benefits that make life pleasant for them. It is good to learn all we can about child psychology and child management, so that we may have wisdom for the great task that lies before us. But more important than these is the gift to our children of that outgoing, overflowing, undemanding quality of love which is continuously generated within a really happy marriage. In this kind of emotional atmosphere a child feels happy and secure. Knowing that his parents truly love him and love each other, he feels beneath him a stable foundation upon which he can completely rely. In this knowledge he can meet the world with courage and with confidence.

When we work to achieve success in marriage, we are thinking chiefly of our own happiness. Yet when two married people, by patient and sustained effort, win through to harmony and peace, they may actually be doing more for their children than they do for themselves.

Part Three

Five
Difficult Partners

CHAPTER XI

THE "FRIGID" WIFE

In the chapter on sex all the emphasis was placed on the positive attainment of a normal, satisfying relationship. However, difficulties can and do arise, as every marriage counselor knows. In this chapter we shall discuss what is probably the most frequently encountered sex difficulty in marriage.

Let me begin by quoting a letter I once received from a wise middle-aged woman. She wrote:

During the past thirty years I have had frank discussions with married women of all ages. When I asked the direct question, "Do you enjoy complete satisfaction through normal sexual intercourse?" the majority answered, "No."

When asked what they were doing about the problem, in most cases they were doing nothing. Fear or despair had paralyzed their capacity for action. There was the wife who just believed she wasn't normal, and felt badly about it; the wife who felt it was dangerous to deflate a man's ego over sex, so she acted a part which did not represent the truth. There were those who had been honest and admitted to their husbands how they felt—only to be labeled "frigid."

Surely, in an enlightened age like ours, we could find a sane, acceptable solution of this dilemma.

First we must get this problem into proper perspective. How many married women really are involved in this kind of difficulty? Both the Kinsey research in the United States and the Chesser inquiry in Britain would suggest that only a minority of wives have trouble in achieving orgasm. So my correspondent was probably given an exaggerated picture of the frequency of the problem.

I do not think, however, that her picture of the intensity of the problem for many wives who encounter it is exaggerated. Over a period of many years I have received a steady stream of letters on this subject. In my work as a marriage counselor it has been a steadily recurring problem. I have frequently encountered in women the exasperation, misery, and despair which my correspondent describes.

In discussions of this problem I do not like the use of the word "frigid." That is why I put it as a quotation in the chapter title. It is a word that carries with it a flavor of judgment, of contempt. Anyway, I consider it to be an inaccurate term in this connection. There *are* women who lack completely any capacity for sexual response. But in these days, when the decision is entirely in their own hands, I don't believe such women are at all likely to marry.

A more accurate term is "orgasm inadequacy." As I have indicated, most wives seem to have little difficulty in achieving orgasm. They may not do so on *every* occasion. Most women are somewhat temperamental in the matter of sexual response. The mood they are in, the general atmosphere, the time of the day or of the month—circumstantial factors of this kind may affect them deeply. But any wife who reaches the climax on most occasions may be described as adequate in this respect.

At the other extreme there is the wife who has *never* experienced orgasm. She may not be at all distressed about this— unless or until her husband begins to pester her with the idea that she isn't functioning as a normal woman should.

It is a mistake to think that these women are cold and unresponsive by nature. On the contrary, they are often deeply affectionate and capable of giving and receiving tender love. It is just that, for them, the mechanism of orgasm doesn't work. This does not necessarily deter them, however, from enjoying sex relations with their husbands. In their quiet way they respond to the warmth and intimacy and closeness of the sexual embrace. Provided they understand the strength and urgency of their husbands' sexual needs and meet them with understanding, and provided their husbands don't pester and harry them about their incapacity to reach the climax, these women can achieve quite happy marriages.

There are, indeed, some women who not only don't achieve orgasm but who have a positive aversion to the sex relationship. This nearly always stems from negative influence in early life which has produced deep-seated feelings of fear or shame or guilt associated with sex. Sometimes it takes extended psychological treatment to get at the root of these feelings. It is always worth while to seek such treatment.

The more common problem associated with orgasm inadequacy, however, is that of the wife who is capable of being aroused to a high pitch of sexual response and who greatly desires the orgasm, but who in spite of every effort reaches the desired goal only very occasionally or not at all.

This situation is highly discouraging to both husband and wife. They make repeated efforts, most of which end in failure. A vicious circle may be set up which results in the difficulty becoming increasingly acute. The husband gets impatient with his wife's inadequacy and may adopt an attitude of contempt and criticism. The wife gets tangled up emotionally and approaches the sex relationship in such a state of apprehension that its natural spontaneity is completely destroyed. Finally she comes to hate and dread the whole business and goes to elaborate lengths to avoid it. This state of affairs can end a marriage.

The fault may lie in the husband's poor technique. We have already discussed the need for him to be willing to wait for his wife's full response. This factor in the sex relationship of married people is much better understood today than it was a few years ago. But we still encounter men whose ignorance of the art of love-making is profound. Fortunately there are now books which can help such a husband to see where he has been going wrong. Better still, he can talk the situation over with a marriage counselor and quickly learn to remedy his former deficiencies.

One lesson he may have to learn is that some women are limited in their capacity for sexual response. A good many, for example, never reach the climax at all without direct stimulation of the clitoris, which is sexually a more responsive organ than the vagina. It may indeed be impossible for the wife to receive the necessary amount of stimulation during sexual union, and the husband may have to use his fingers to bring his wife to the point of orgasm, either before or after his own climax has been reached.

Some wives, also, are only capable of full sexual response at certain times during their monthly cycle or under certain other circumstances peculiar to themselves. Where there is mutual understanding, the wife can explain this to her husband. Yet it is surprising how often, out of false modesty or embarrassment, a wife will fail to do so.

It may be, however, that the husband's technique leaves nothing to be desired. He is informed, considerate, and patient. Yet his wife, eagerly desiring to reach the climax, cannot in spite of all his help manage to do so.

In such a situation as this it is almost certain that the wife is "emotionally blocked," as the psychologists put it. On the surface, and at the moment, she strongly desires to achieve orgasm. But there is somewhere in her mind a hidden restraint, a brake that holds her back. This is almost always an attitude of anxiety about sex—not as strong as that which we find in the wife who has a revulsion against the sex relationship, but strong enough to hinder her at the critical point at which she would otherwise reach the climax. She may not be consciously aware of this state of affairs. That is what makes the problem so baffling to her. But somewhere in her background, as a result of some earlier experience or influence, she has developed a negative attitude—an inhibition—toward her own sexual functioning.

In a few cases this inhibition produces a condition known as vaginismus. The wife, gripped by deep-seated fear or anxiety, tightens up her muscles as her husband approaches her. The result is that it is impossible for him to penetrate, and intercourse cannot take place. She does not do this deliberately. She cannot indeed control her reaction. Intellectually she may wish to relax and respond. But her emotions take over and she can do nothing about it.

Wives thwarted by orgasm inadequacy should seek the aid of a marriage counselor, who will refer them if necessary for psychological help. The outlook for these cases is often quite good. The very fact that the wife feels so strongly the desire to reach the orgasm, and often gets so near to it, suggests that with the right kind of readjustment at the appropriate point, the break-through may be achieved. But the longer a couple in this predicament delay seeking help, the more complex the emotional situation becomes, and the more difficult in consequence is the counselor's task.

Men rarely suffer from orgasm inadequacy. A husband may, however, develop a condition called impotence, which is very humiliating to him because he finds himself unable to achieve or maintain the state of erection which is necessary if he is to penetrate his wife. This condition is the counterpart of vaginismus in the wife, in that it is usually the result of an unconscious anxiety about his sexual desires. The help of a marriage counselor should always be sought when this is encountered. There is little chance that the couple will be able to deal with the problem by themselves.

The wife who has difficulty in achieving sexual response should always realize that this creates a problem for her husband as well as for herself. It is very hard for a man to be denied by his wife. It piles up in him a fierce intensity of resentment and frustration that may drive him almost to the point of desperation. A loving wife will never allow this to happen if she understands how deeply her man suffers. Even if she is not capable of responding fully, she can usually in some way contrive to give her husband relief, and so earn his gratitude. Nothing dries up affection and tenderness in a husband more decisively than a sexual rebuff from his wife.

If the sexual life of a married couple isn't satisfactory, there are three steps they can take. First, if at all possible, they should talk it over frankly together, with all cards on the table. If this doesn't help, they should study together some sound books on the subject. If the trouble still persists, they should take the problem to a marriage counselor. The benefits of good sex adjustment are too great to be missed by any couple who sincerely wish their marriage to succeed.

CHAPTER XII

THE SILENT HUSBAND

We have a tradition that women are great talkers. It is well expressed in the inn sign with the title "The Silent Woman." The accompanying picture explains all. The unhappy lady has been deprived of her head!

What lies behind this idea? Surely men talk a great deal. As far as I can recall, all the great orators in history have been men. Even today, with equality of opportunity, men seem easily to outshine women in public speaking.

As I have considered this, I have come to the conclusion that the real difference lies not in the extent to which men and women talk but in the use to which they put the function of speech. When men talk, they are expressing ideas. When women talk, they are expressing feelings.

Of course that's a generalization. But I think it furnishes us with some valuable clues for the understanding of ourselves and of one another.

When a woman is in a state of strong emotion, she has the impulse to talk. She feels more secure and gains relief by letting her feelings come out. She expresses love and discharges hate.

A man under the stress of emotion doesn't want to talk. His impulse is to lapse into silence. He closes the gate, pulls up the drawbridge, and retreats into himself.

The man may, in fact, find the woman's need for expression disturbing. Rupert Brooke pictures the man lost in reverie in the contemplation of nature, when the woman breaks into the silence with some prosaic remark about how pretty it is. Infuriated, the spell broken, the man cries, "You came and quacked beside me in the wood!"

When the woman expresses hostile emotion, the man is no match for her. It is not a matter of chance that the woman's ultimate weapon—nagging—is launched by word of mouth.

What is the reason for this difference between the sexes? I am inclined to think that it is largely a matter of conditioning. In countries where traditions of courage and toughness in the male are strong, boys are trained from their earliest years in strict emotional control. While the small girl may cry freely when she feels like it, her brother is enjoined to keep a stiff upper lip and not to behave like a baby. As the boy grows older, the one thing he knows his peers will never forgive or forget is any manifestation of softness or emotion. When he learns to box, it is impressed upon him that however much he is hurt he mustn't show it, because that will be a signal to his adversary to wade in and finish him off.

So we carefully breed a race of men who keep their emotions battened down. The type of man we admire is the "strong, silent" type. By linking together these two concepts of silence and strength, we reveal that we really equate them.

All cultures do not follow the same pattern. Men of the Latin countries, for example, are much more free emotionally. They express their feelings volubly, they embrace each other, they weep when vexed. Sometimes we treat these strange antics with indulgence. But most of the time, somewhere deep down, we are contemptuous of them. Real men, we say to ourselves, don't act like that. The man who isn't silent can't really be strong.

The wife who finds her husband's silences baffling would do well to remember all this. Her man through long years has been trained to act thus. Whenever feelings rise within him, welling up with such force that they clamor for expression, his automatic response is to choke them back, especially in the presence of a woman. To lash out in anger at a woman is un-chivalrous. To cry in a woman's presence is contemptible. What is to be done, therefore, except to beat a retreat, to get away by himself until he can gain control of his feelings again?

An ex-Army man once told me, in the manner of one confidentially imparting sound advice, that he had learned the secret of handling all disagreements that developed between himself and his wife. Whenever there arose any sign of trouble brewing, he said, he would abruptly rise, get his hat from the hall, leave the house, and take a long walk. On his return an hour or so later, he declared triumphantly, the subject of the threatened controversy was not again referred to.

This man was taking a characteristically masculine line of action. He would probably have been astonished if I had suggested that his behavior must have been maddening to his wife, because what she wanted to do was to talk the issue out and in that way to achieve an exchange of feelings about it.

The average husband doesn't go to the trouble of fetching his hat from the hall. He learns instead to pull down an invisible curtain that shuts out his wife, to assume a sphinxlike indifference to all that she says and does. This is powerfully effective. Often I have noted the desperation in a woman's eyes as she has said, "I can't make any headway at all. You see, my husband doesn't talk!"

What can a wife do in this predicament?

The most useless course she can take is to try to break through the man's defenses. This she usually finds out quickly enough.

The more vigorously she attacks him, the more deeply he retreats within his shell.

A far better plan is for her to consider carefully just what is happening, and why.

The strange truth is that when a man has to retreat into silence before his wife, he experiences a sense of deep disappointment. This is in fact the last thing he wanted to do.

Men are ready enough to bottle up their emotions in the presence of each other and in the day-to-day life of the world. But every normal man longs for a relationship so private and so intimate that he may let his guard down and release his pent-up feelings freely and safely. It is his dream that he can enter into this kind of intimacy and trust with the woman he loves. When he finds himself unable to do this, he is deeply disillusioned.

What he really wants is some relief from the strict and incessant control of his emotions which the culture has imposed upon him. But he can do little to bring this about of his own accord. He looks to the woman, who has not been subject to the stern disciplines laid upon him, to unlock the doors of his heart, to remove the "taboo on tenderness" (as Ian Suttie so expressively called it), and to lead him into a new experience of emotional freedom.

It is therefore the wife's task to draw her husband out of the abyss of silence in which his deepest feelings become entombed. It may not be an easy task. It may require much patience and sympathy and insight. Yet it is a task for which every true woman is by her feminine nature well equipped. At this point, more deeply perhaps than at any other, the wife has to be a mother to her man. For what she has to do is to re-create for him the warm and confiding relationship he knew with his mother before the masculine world to which he belonged took him over and began to toughen him and make him into a man.

The wife who can do this for her husband will earn his undying gratitude and devotion. This is one of the things he wants most from his marriage—to be able to break through his silences and to share his deepest feelings, and, having done so, to be understood and comforted and healed. The woman who can do this for her man truly wins his heart, for he has confided to her the secret of his innermost self, which he has closely kept from all the rest of the world. In the perfect romances of the fairy tales, this was dramatized when the Prince sat down with the Princess and "told her all his heart." It is not easy for any man to do this. Yet it is what he wants to do with a deep and desperate longing.

When once a man's confidence has been gained by his wife, she will find that his silences were only a defense. Given the right opportunity, a man wants to talk just as much as a woman does, in order to express his feelings. In addition, he has another need stronger than hers—a need to talk about his ideas, his dreams, his plans, his ambitions. In talking thus he clears his mind, advances his thought, resolves his problems. As Edward Carpenter put it, he thinks of his wife as the trusted comrade "into whose mind his thoughts naturally flow, as it were to know themselves and to receive a new illumination."

The wife who finds that her husband won't talk may have a difficult man on her hands and may deserve our pity. But it may be, too, that she has not clearly understood one of her supreme tasks as a wife and has therefore failed to accomplish it. In many areas in the complex interaction between the husband and the wife, the initiative belongs to the husband, and he must take the lead. But in the area of putting deep feelings into words, the woman is generally much better qualified than her inhibited and tongue-tied consort. Here, in most marriages, he will welcome her encouragement and help, her understanding and acceptance.

If the husband doesn't talk, therefore, it may be safely assumed that it isn't because he doesn't want to talk or because he has nothing to say. It is rather that he is too fearful, too unsure of himself, too distrustful of his partner, to open the heavy fastenings of the door of his heart. This presents a problem which every wife must meet in her own way. It is not for me, a man, to tell a woman how to be a woman. But what I can tell her is that, if she succeeds in this and wins her husband's complete confidence and total trust, the success of her marriage will be assured.

CHAPTER XIII

THE NAGGING WIFE

"When I first married her, Gwen was such a nice girl—sweet and pleasant," said Stanley wearily. "But all that is a thing of the past. I don't know why it is, but she seems to have changed completely. Now she does nothing but nag, nag, nag from morning till night. It's getting me down, and I tell you, I can't take it much longer."

Stanley's complaint has been echoed by tens of thousands of disillusioned husbands. When polls are taken to discover what unhappily married men and women object to in each other, nagging on the wife's part almost always heads the male list.

Later, when I saw Gwen and confronted her with the fact that her marriage was hanging by a thread, she admitted that she nagged Stanley.

"But why do I do it?" she cried. "I really don't know."

That would seem to be an important question. I went to my bookshelves and took down at random ten books on marriage. Only one had "nagging" in the index at all—and what it said on the subject would have been no help at all to poor Gwen.

I tried the dictionary. I learned that "to nag" is "to scold, find fault, or urge continually." Not very helpful! The derivation of the word, however, seemed to me significant. It comes from the Anglo-Saxon "gnagan," which means "to gnaw."

That was all that the books could offer. So I sat down and thought of some of the marriage problems I had dealt with in which nagging was a factor—how it had arisen and what the wives and husbands had said about it. Slowly the pattern emerged.

Nagging, in the first place, is essentially a woman's weapon. I have very seldom heard of a man who nagged. Moreover, it seems to be a weapon which women use, not against each other, but against men. And generally it is used in the marriage relationship. So pre-eminently nagging is a procedure employed by the woman in her role as wife.

But *why* do wives nag? That was Gwen's question.

Over long periods of human history, wives have had to use this weapon because often it was the only one they had. Until very recent times, the woman has been in a subservient position to the man—first because he was physically stronger, and later because he also had cultural authority and economic power over her.

So the woman must soon have learned that a direct frontal attack upon the lordly male wasn't likely to achieve anything. The only way to gain her ends was to embark on a long siege, use guerrilla tactics, and fight a war of attrition. The method was to introduce into the man's life a recurrent irritation—a gnawing pain like the toothache, which slowly wore him down until he was ready to give in for the sake of peace. It was the technique of the water dripping relentlessly on the stone.

It is an eminently successful technique if your aim is to get something you want. If you go pestering a man and he can't slam the door in your face, or hang up the phone, or walk out and leave you, he'll probably capitulate in the end. Of course you don't overdo it at any given time. The art of nagging is that you never keep it up long enough to create an explosion. As the danger point approaches, you stop, then come back to it again later. You keep up this procedure till your husband finally gives in.

Nagging may seem to be justified when a husband is close-fisted, obdurate, and inconsiderate. A wife has certain inalienable rights, and when her man refuses to yield them to her, he no doubt deserves what he gets. Yet it is a sad state of affairs when marriage descends to that sort of level. A wife who resorts to nagging is rather like a husband who resorts to violence. Each is falling back on a primitive weapon. This is in its very nature an admission of defeat, an abandonment of more civilized means.

What does nagging really accomplish? It achieves the wife's individual purpose at the expense of the relationship. That was how it worked out for Gladys. She didn't like city life and grumbled about it until Peter, in desperation, agreed to give up the apartment and travel in to town every day from a country cottage. But Peter, though he gave in, resented the long journeys involved. So he felt justified in staying the night in town more and more often, and it was in this way that he became involved in the affair that finally ended his marriage.

No husband can continue to feel affectionate toward a wife who nags him. He isn't persuaded that he is wrong. He capitulates out of exasperation. And in the process there is a loss of the feeling of tenderness, a hardening of the heart, toward his wife. So the wife who begins to nag may find that she has to go on nagging. It becomes the only method she can use to get anything. And as the husband's resentment increases, he becomes more stubborn and holds out longer. So the wife has to nag more and more, until it becomes habitual for her to do so.

Marjorie was like that. Her voice, when she spoke to Fred, was a cross between a whine and a threat. Thirty years of marriage had made her a most unpleasant person. And Fred had developed toward her, by long practice in dogged resistance, a hide like that of a rhinoceros. It was a wonder, the neighbors said, that they stayed together. Once those two had been in love, but no one could now imagine such a thing between them.

Nagging, then, is best thought of as a last-ditch weapon, to be used only in emergency situations and with a full awareness of the dangers involved. A wife can do almost nothing more calculated to alienate her husband's affections.

But if Gwen is to give up nagging, what is her alternative? Is she to make herself into a doormat, subjugating her will completely to that of Stanley and surrendering all her individual rights and needs?

Not at all. Here are some practical suggestions which I would offer to a wife who is tempted to embark upon a nagging campaign. Let's say she has decided that she wants her husband to buy her a fur coat.

1. Are you really quite convinced that this is a reasonable request to make at this time, in relation to your husband's income and the other demands upon the family budget? Is this something he really is in a position to give you, or are you exploiting him?

2. If your conclusion is that it *is* a reasonable request, have you tried to think out carefully how you can present the case to your husband in terms that are clear, cogent, and convincing? A man is always impressed by a well-thought-out argument, persuasively presented. The nature of nagging is that it is sheer pressure, with little or no logical persuasion behind it.

3. Do you recognize the wisdom of choosing the right occasion to make this request to your husband? A wise woman sees the importance of getting her man in the right mood before she presents some new proposition. For instance, it wouldn't be sensible to bring up the subject when he is tired or discouraged

or when he has just paid the household bills and remarked how high they were last month!

4. Have you considered the possibility of doing a little bargaining? If you do something for him that he has wanted very much or offer to help him out in some difficult situation, then your request may seem a fair return and a special way in which he can express his gratitude.

5. If, despite the fact that you are convinced of the reasonableness of your request, your husband can't be persuaded to grant it and can't give you acceptable reasons for the refusal, may it be that your marriage needs some critical evaluation? Is it possible that your husband doesn't love you as much as he once did or as much as you thought he did? If not, why not? Maybe you'd better find out.

The truth is that a woman who knows how to make her man happy can wield a tremendous influence over him. The man who loves his wife tenderly will not, within reason, be able to refuse her anything. So the nagging wife is really a self-confessed failure as a wife. She has failed to make her man feel so pleased and proud and grateful that he will jump at the chance to do something for her that will give her special pleasure.

Nagging, then, is a woman's weapon. But it is not a weapon that a woman would need to use who is succeeding as a woman. When she has to use it, even if she does so successfully, it is the symbol of her tragedy and despair. For the fact that she has to nag her husband indicates that, in the deepest sense, they have ceased—or never learned—to love each other.

CHAPTER XIV

THE UNFAITHFUL HUSBAND

"It was a terrible shock to me," said Ann, "when I found out about Tony and this other woman. It just stunned me, and I felt for a while that the bottom had dropped out of my world.

"I still feel like that. I think and think—but my thoughts are completely overwhelmed by my feelings—anger, disillusionment, and self-pity. I'm all mixed up. What should I do next? I really don't know."

This is an experience which most wives expect never to go through. But when it does hit a woman, it is liable to hit her very hard indeed.

And the chances that it may happen are not, alas, so infinitesimal that they can be ignored. The circumstances in which we live today tend to make marital infidelity easier than it was in the past. There is more opportunity for it and less censure when it happens. The Kinsey research considers it safe to assume that half of all American husbands have been unfaithful at some time during their marriage. Even if we halve the figure, that is one in four. And even if it were only one in ten, that would be reason enough for many wives to face, however reluctantly, the possibility. "I never dreamed that this would happen to me"—these are perhaps the most common opening words that the marriage counselor hears. And even if it couldn't happen to you, it might happen to your best friend, and she might put to you the question that Ann put to me. What would be your answer?

The law treats all acts of adultery alike—at least as grounds admissible in matrimonial suits. In personal relationships, however, this can blur the real issues. I do not mean to condone infidelity. But my experience as a counselor convinces me that there can be a casual incident that really does not arise out of a basic pattern of infidelity and that ought not to be treated at all in the same category as more serious affairs.

More than one man has confessed to me a lapse that was the result of a momentary, unpremeditated temptation that threw him temporarily off balance. This is much more likely to happen to a man than to a woman. He may be driven into a casual encounter out of idle curiosity or a passing desire for variety. He may be tired or lonely or may have had too much to drink. He may be put under social pressure by irresponsible companions. Remember, such an encounter can for a man be almost unbelievably superficial. For him there is no risk of pregnancy involved, and there may be no depth of relationship implied.

This is hard for some women to understand. When the contrite husband assures his wife that what he has done hasn't affected his love for her in the slightest, she may consider this a monstrous insult. Yet it may literally be true. In such a case, matters are only made far worse when the wife insists on making a big issue of it and belaboring her husband till their relationship really *does* become strained on his side. When the wife is satisfied that the incident was a momentary lapse for which her husband really is sorry, the wise course is to dismiss it without further elaboration. For this the husband will be duly grateful.

But infidelity may be something far more serious than that. The wife may find that she has been replaced by another. Then she really faces a crisis. She is concerned not with something her husband has done and for which he is now ashamed and sorry, but with a *person*—another woman, who confronts her as a rival for her husband's affection and as a threat to her marriage.

A woman's basic reaction to this experience is to suffer an overwhelming sense of insecurity. Ann expressed this by saying that the bottom had dropped out of her world. Her predominant emotions—anger, disillusionment, self-pity—though very different from each other, all derived from this underlying sense of insecurity. She was shocked and shattered to realize that she was expendable.

Unless her husband is a wanton philanderer, back at his old tricks, the wife had better try to keep her head and ask herself some searching questions. This is hard, because her first strong impulse is to feel so hurt and let down that she wants to fly off the handle. But that won't help at all. Her husband knows quite well that he is doing wrong. He's been living with that awareness ever since the affair started. And by now he has summoned up all the excuses he can muster to drown the voice of conscience. The chance that his wife can penetrate his defenses at this point, by telling him aggressively what he has known perfectly well all along, is not good.

In fact, the way an unfaithful husband usually steels himself is to say that his wife is lacking in understanding. This is what he tells the other woman and what he tells himself. So when his wife turns on him with all the fury of a woman scorned, his attempt to persuade himself that she is really an unpleasant person is heavily reinforced, and he is propelled yet further away from her and toward the other woman.

I am not implying, of course, that a wife should not feel indignant. My point is that, before she explodes emotionally, she should try to do some serious thinking. In most cases when a man turns away from his wife to another woman, he is looking for something he has missed in his marriage. This doesn't excuse what he does. But it helps to explain what he does.

Sometimes the husband was sexually frustrated. He may not have said so, because the modern husband does not force his attentions on his wife. But if she is inhibited or lacking in warm responsiveness, he secretly takes this as a rebuff. Margaret was scarcely aware that her rather prim and prudish attitude made any real difference to her relationship with Frank. Her impassioned protest, when she discovered his secret attachment, was "But what can a man of Frank's intelligence see in a woman so—so cheap and sensual?" It was not easy for her to come to terms with the fact that what he saw in her was precisely what he had failed to find in his wife.

Or the husband may have felt lonely and uncared for. His wife may have been so efficiently busy that she had no time to be tender and comforting to him. She may have made no effort to make herself attractive. Whatever it was, he was made aware that some need was not being met in his marriage. Then someone else appeared who offered to fill the vacuum.

At first he was wishing all the time that this actually *was* his wife. I have been impressed by the number of husbands who have said this. And sometimes it could easily have been so, because the wife was just as charming, just as intelligent, potentially just as attractive. But he met his wife only in the dull routine of the home, and all they talked about was how the children had misbehaved and how they were going to manage to pay the bills. His secret meetings with the other woman, dressed up to please him and flattering him with her sympathetic attention and fulsome admiration, were an exhilarating escape from the dull boredom to which marriage had degenerated.

A wife who is objective enough to see at least the possibility of this can make a deep impression on her erring husband. "I'll never forget," said Jim, "how Alice behaved when my sordid little affair with the girl at the office blew up in her face. I knew it must be hurting her terribly—but she didn't whine and she didn't lash out. She sat me down, looked me straight in the eyes, and asked me where she had gone wrong and what this girl had that she hadn't. In that moment I knew what a fine person Alice really was, and I felt ashamed of the whole business. From that moment the other girl didn't have a chance."

It isn't always as easy as this, by any means. But the fundamental truth which any wife must face when she finds her husband unfaithful is that she has a *competitor* to deal with. Of course the wife can insist on her rights and line up an army of friends and relatives to batter the husband into submission. Sometimes this works. But it is a shallow victory at best. The real reason that he failed her remains unfaced, and it may quite possibly be that in the first place she had failed him. What this wife has done is to defeat her rival, not by proving her love to be the greater but by proving her armament to be the stronger. She has recaptured her husband outwardly—but it does not follow that she has won back his heart.

This may, of course, be better than nothing. And in time he may come around. Meanwhile, the wife has ensured her economic security. Yet even this is not always so. In the world of today pressures of this kind are proving less and less effective to restrain the erring husband. We may deplore this—but the wife, in her own interests, had better recognize it.

Now as of old, the true inner bond that sustains a marriage is love—not a superficial sentiment, but a deep, sustained, outgoing concern for the loved one. In times past this was often obscured by the strong external ties that held a marriage together regardless of its internal quality. But as these external ties progressively weaken, the importance of the inner bond of love stands ever more clearly revealed.

When a husband has been unfaithful, this is a challenge to the wife to demonstrate the reality, not of her power, but of her love. It is a test of love's quality—its integrity, its strength, its depth. To say that even love at its highest and best can save a marriage when a rival has already entered the picture would be promising too much. But at least this can be said. If all the resources that love can command cannot save the marriage, certainly nothing else can.

CHAPTER XV

THE AGING WIFE

At some indeterminate point following her fortieth birthday the average wife experiences a feeling of emotional disturbance. It varies between one woman and another in intensity. For some it amounts to little more than a vague sense of insecurity and wistfulness. For others it seems like a catastrophic presentiment of impending doom.

Anyone who has talked much with women passing through this period of their lives becomes aware that there may be three causes of this disturbed feeling. Any one of these is enough to produce it. Sometimes two of them, and sometimes all three, will coincide.

The first is the awareness of the woman that she has completed, or almost completed, her reproductive task. Nature has provided the birds and animals with a convenient mechanism which causes them to lose interest in their young, and even chase them away, when dependence upon the mother is no longer necessary. But if this instinct has any vestiges remaining in the human mother, it has been overlaid by the strong, deep, and extended association with her children which the complexity of our culture requires of her. It is only a feckless and irresponsible woman who can relinquish her children, when the time comes, without a pang.

So the experience of the "empty nest" is always something of a crisis. It leaves a devastating sense of emptiness and purposelessness. The silent house is full of memories. There was once so much to do, and now there is so little. The crowded, busy years seemed arduous at the time. But now, looking back, it is clear that this was far outweighed by the deep, solid satisfaction of being needed.

And so, as she turns her eyes to the future, the mother realizes that—barring emergencies—her children will never really need her again. As she becomes aware of this, she recognizes that at least half of the meaning has gone out of life for her. Where can she find a new sense of purpose to take the place of the one that is now fulfilled?

The insecure wife has no answer. Her response is to cling to her children, to refuse to let them go. She showers them with indulgences in a pathetic attempt to earn their gratitude, champions them needlessly against imaginary threats, and resents bitterly anyone else to whom they may transfer their dependence or allegiance. These are the ingredients that produce the interfering mother-in-law. Invariably she is an insecure woman who has failed to accept herself or to make her marriage a deeply satisfying relationship. Without realizing it she is trying to exploit her grown-up children in the desperate attempt to fortify her own failing self-esteem.

The second cause of disturbance in the aging wife is the painful awareness of what is happening to her. Of course it is true that all of us are growing old all the time. But the process is generally gradual enough not to shock us, except occasionally when we turn over a bundle of old photographs and see vividly what the hand of time has wrought.

There is, however, for the woman a particular point of crisis within this natural process. It is the point at which she looks in the mirror and knows that her feminine charm is slipping away forever. This may not be strictly true—but that is how she interprets it. Consciously or unconsciously, most women derive a good deal of their self-confidence from the fact that as women they seem desirable in men's eyes. Even the girl who affects to scorn the eager curiosity of the casual male is secretly comforted by the awareness that she is worth a second glance. This is not vanity or superficiality. It is a basic element in the psychology of a normal, natural woman.

For the wife this feeling about herself is linked with the security of her marriage. She knows that a major element in holding her man is keeping herself desirable in his eyes. The world as she knows it is full of predatory females ready to catch unwary husbands off their guard.

This means that the decline in her attractiveness may mean the shattering of her security. The graying hair, the spreading wrinkles, the flattening curves of her body—these are the manifestations of her devaluation as currency in the social market. With a start she realizes that the man who is looking in her direction isn't looking at her. He is looking past her to the bright young thing at the other end of the room. With a sinking heart she wonders when her husband will be doing the same.

I have expressed this a little crudely. Not all wives are thus troubled. Some have enough assets in other directions to know that feminine charm does not depend on firm flesh and a fine figure. Others are so deeply sure of the integrity of their husbands that no real fears assail them. Yet these women differ from the others not in kind, but only, though widely, in degree. Consciously or unconsciously, every wife suffers some deflation of her ego when the tangible tokens of her feminine attractiveness pass from her. However gracefully she makes the adjustment, an adjustment is involved. And it is an adjustment necessitated by a retreat, a straightening of the line of battle after territory has been yielded to the enemy.

For many women, indeed, the whole idea of making a strategic withdrawal is intolerable. We live in an era when youth is extolled as unreasonably as age is despised. The honor and respect once paid naturally to advancing years is now grudgingly accorded. Indeed, the older person who is most honored is often the one who contrives to cheat nature. "Isn't she marvelous for her age? She looks at least ten years younger than she is!" "He's a grand old man. He can still keep up with chaps half his age!"

So the desperate aging wife struggles to keep young. She calls to her aid all the resources she can command—cosmetics and calisthenics, dress and diet. The great deception is sustained as long as possible. But inevitably the moment of full realization, which she has fought off with desperate gallantry, must come. Its postponement doesn't help, for adjustments are only harder to make after they have been fiercely resented and fought off. The mood of acceptance makes growing old easier than does the desperation of defeat.

The third strand in the pattern of the middle-aged wife's anxiety is the onset of the menopause—the "change of life." I have deliberately put this last, because it is often blamed for much more than it is responsible for. Husbands confide knowingly to their close friends that their wives are proving awkward to live with because they are going through a "difficult period in a woman's life." They say it with a confident air which implies that they can't and needn't do anything about it. By attributing it all to the wife's bodily chemistry they conveniently unload the responsibility for dealing with it onto the doctor.

Without doubt the glandular readjustments involved in the termination of the woman's reproductive function have their emotional repercussions. These are sometimes mild, sometimes violent, sometimes brief, sometimes extended. But I am convinced that many of the symptoms of panic, of depression, of irrational and impulsive behavior, which are observed in middle-aged wives are due more to the traumatic effects of the empty nest and of the awareness of growing old than to the reproductive glands signing off duty. And I believe that if husbands understood this clearly and entered more sympathetically into the woman's experience, they could help their wives immensely in the adjustments with which they are faced.

In fact, the crisis through which the aging wife passes is really in the end a crisis in her marriage. At each point in her task of adjustment her relationship with her husband can be, and should be, the stabilizing factor.

Parting with your children is inevitably hard. But for the contented couple it brings solid compensations. The wife who is no longer preoccupied with her children's needs has more time to give to her husband. As a rule he is in the full tide of his powers, working hard and carrying responsibility. Now his wife is more free than she has been for years—free to give him comfort, comradeship, and all kinds of practical help. Meals à deux provide the opportunity for those deep, intimate talks that were always being crowded out in the more tumultuous years. The couple have new freedom to undertake new enterprises—to travel together, to take up old hobbies or to develop new ones. The later years of marriage need not imply stagnation. They may become in their own way the best years of all. The empty nest can be made a very cozy corner where the erstwhile parents rest contentedly after their labors.

Likewise, growing old need not be viewed as a disaster. There are encouraging signs that the distorted doctrine of golden youth being the only coinage which can buy happiness is giving place to a more balanced view. The great extension of life expectancy and of leisure time which science is bestowing upon us all—and especially upon the married woman—is making us aware that the late afternoon can be one of the most pleasant and satisfying periods in the life span. If middle age means coming in out of the open sea and resting in the shallows, we may remind ourselves that the lagoon offers warmth and calm which are welcome indeed to those who have wrestled long enough with the breakers.

The menopause, too, brings its blessings. Why maintain a function whose purpose has been fulfilled? The passing of the reproductive powers brings a simplification of living. It is the inward equivalent of moving out of the big house which was needed to accommodate the children and settling in a more compact and workable bungalow. Nothing essential is lost. It is a fallacious error that the end of a woman's reproductive life implies the end of her sexual life. Often, indeed, this part of her marriage comes to be more satisfying than ever, when every lurking fear of the unwanted pregnancy can be completely eliminated. I recall the story of the curious girl who ventured to ask a sweet old lady in her seventies at what age a wife lost interest in the sex relationship. With a gracious smile she replied, "My dear, you'll have to ask someone much older than I am. I just don't know!"

Middle age is in fact one of life's major transition periods. Like adolescence it is the passage of the personality from one major phase to another. This involves losses. It also involves gains. To shrink from the change, to try to continue to live in the former phase, is a futile waste of effort. To defy the tempest and march bravely on is to pass swiftly through to the tranquillity beyond.

To the wife who faces middle age and its implications, the best advice that can be given is—"Keep your marriage in good repair." For if she has held her husband's love and won his wholehearted devotion, the threefold change of the middle years need hold no terrors.

Part Four

Five Perplexing Problems

CHAPTER XVI

JEALOUSY

"What am I supposed to do," Margaret challenged, "when another girl throws her arms round my husband at a party and kisses him? Fred says I take things like that far too seriously." She paused and then went on. "Well, I suppose he's right. If Helen really had designs on Fred, she wouldn't have given herself away in public. But I can't help my feelings. I just boiled over.

"All right. I'm a jealous wife. But I don't like being that way. What can I do about it?"

Jealousy can be a very destructive force in a marriage. Yet we won't understand it aright unless we recognize at the start that it is essentially quite natural and, in its right place, good and useful.

We are all endowed with certain protective emotions. Fear is one—it makes you careful as you cross a busy street. Anxiety is another—it makes you prepare carefully that speech you have to make, so that when the time comes, you do full justice to yourself. Jealousy is a third—it makes you watchful over the relationships upon which your security and happiness depend.

If Helen really *did* have designs on Fred, Margaret's marriage would be in danger. In such a situation it would be unnatural for Margaret to remain calm and indifferent. It would be *necessary* for her to be disturbed, just as you ought to be disturbed when you discover that the house is on fire. Jealousy is the emotion that triggers off the disturbance that gets you moving into the appropriate course of action.

Daphne, for instance, was justified in keeping a close watch on Peter after his affair with Janet. He didn't like being questioned about his movements for several months following their reconciliation. But he had betrayed Daphne's trust, and he couldn't complain because she remained on the alert until he had given her convincing proof of his genuine repentance.

However, our protective emotions can easily get out of hand. Then they trigger us into a state of disturbance which has no real justification. This was Fred's complaint about Margaret's violent reaction to the party incident. There was nothing in it, really. Helen was an old friend with an exuberant disposition and demonstrative habits—that was all. Her kiss of welcome was the equivalent of a hearty handshake from anyone else.

But to Margaret this was ominous. Behind irrational jealousy there is always insecurity. Margaret had been widowed at twenty-three, her husband tragically killed in a flying accident. Left with a child, she saw only emptiness and despair in the future. When Fred offered her his love and protection, it was more than she had dared to hope for. Her happiness was complete.

Then suddenly she saw another woman in Fred's arms, and all the alarm bells rang inside her. She couldn't stop to reason, to hear explanations. All the anguish of the earlier incident when she was widowed surged within her. The voice of panic cried, "Look out, you're going to lose Fred too. Then you'll be finished!"

Fred needed to understand this. Naturally, he interpreted the incident at its face value and saw in Margaret a peevish suspiciousness that he despised. Margaret, however, was not reacting to a trivial incident but to an imminent catastrophe. Her previous tragic experience invested Helen's innocent kiss with the dimensions of disaster.

This is the way irrational jealousy always works. We naturally interpret the incidents of our lives in terms of our previous experiences of a similar kind. The jealous wife reads more into the situation than is really there—for other people. What she reads into it *is* there for her, however. It implies a threat that she is about to suffer a very painful experience—an experience of rejection—that she has suffered before. Her wild, panic-stricken jealousy is a frantic effort to fight off that dire possibility.

If Fred could have understood this, he would have known that laughing at Margaret's fears and complaining of her questioning was not the way to react. She could easily interpret these responses as evasiveness and defensiveness on his part—patterns of behavior that would seem to confirm her fears. What she needed was his comfort and the reassurance of his love.

Yet unfortunately it is true that the actions of an irrationally jealous wife can produce in her husband the very behavior—irritation, impatience, resentment—which appears to confirm her suspicions that he has ceased to love her.

Worse than that. A jealous wife is not an easy or pleasant person to live with. It is miserable to be constantly under suspicion—especially without cause. You don't feel warm and tender toward someone who is constantly spilling out resentment toward you and making false accusations against you. You feel hurt, thwarted, indignant, misunderstood. You feel you want to find someone kind, generous, sympathetic, who will believe in you and comfort and reassure you.

In short, jealousy creates the atmosphere in marriage that encourages the very thing which jealousy suspects. I have known cases in which a wife, jealous of her husband without cause, has driven him by her nagging to create in reality the very situation which at first existed only in her imagination.

The emotion of jealousy, in fact, becomes self-defeating when it gets out of control. This is characteristic of all our protective emotions. Fear is healthy when it makes you watch your step carefully as you cross the road. But it can reach an intensity that causes you to lose your head and rush blindly into the path of a passing car. Anxiety is good if it makes you prepare your speech carefully. But it becomes destructive if it reduces you to a trembling, bewildered, stage-struck bundle of nerves when you face your audience.

As I have explained, jealousy usually gets out of control because it awakens emotional echoes of previous experiences of inadequacy and rejection. This need not be a previous marriage that ended in tragedy, as in Margaret's case. Insecurity in childhood, failure to measure up to what was required of you educationally, socially, or in your work—these and many similar experiences can make you hypersensitive to any threat to your marriage. What prompts irrational jealousy is an ominous little voice inside that says, "Watch out, or some other woman will get your husband. You know you're not all you try to persuade yourself you are. You could easily lose him. Remember how you failed, were turned down, rejected, before. It could happen again."

The fact must be faced that we live in a world where marriages are not as stable as they were, and this fact encourages the insecure wife to yield to panic. We are constantly hearing of men who leave their wives to go off with another woman. Some of them are actually in our circle of friends and acquaintances. Society no longer censures such conduct as it once did.

Consequently the shadow of the other woman is never far away from the anxious, insecure wife.

Most modern women grew up with a vague, underlying awareness that they might have to compete for the available men. They viewed the girls around them as potential rivals. In the old days the rule was that once you had hooked and landed your man, you could relax. Now this is no longer true. The modern wife is geared to an awareness that she must practice eternal vigilance, lest the interloper creep in unawares.

It is easy to see that middle age is a period in a woman's life in which acute jealousy could easily develop. And this is actually the case. It is at this time of life particularly that the wife develops wildly irrational delusions about her husband. Without a shred of evidence she may become convinced that he is carrying on an affair with someone at his work, or some friend or neighbor. She will check on his every movement, go through his pockets, open his letters—to his intense annoyance. What these gestures mean is—"My husband doesn't love me any more, now that I'm getting old and done. There must be another woman in his life." In some cases this lamentable condition becomes so serious that it requires psychiatric treatment.

Of course, men also develop irrational jealousy. All that I have written concerning the wife can be equally true of the husband. In his case too, the cause is the same—deep, haunting, underlying insecurity.

Most of us need a better understanding of jealousy. I find that most married people have never thought it out intelligently and consequently have the most confused ideas on the subject. Needless to say, this doesn't help them to cope with it intelligently when it becomes an issue in their lives.

Handling jealousy in an enlightened way can do a great deal to prevent its otherwise corrosive influence in a marriage. If the root cause of the jealousy cannot be traced, it would be wise to seek the help of a marriage counselor or psychiatrist. We don't have to live in the dark about our emotions when available help could let in the light.

CHAPTER XVII

RELIGIOUS DIFFERENCES

All over the world today interfaith marriages appear to be on the increase. This is not surprising. Everywhere the age-old barriers which have separated people from one another are going down. In contrast to the old world, where prejudice kept the adherents of different religious groups at a safe and suspicious distance from each other, the modern trend is for them to meet in a spirit of tolerant and cordial respect for each other's convictions.

This new spirit is all to the good insofar as it promotes the peaceful coexistence of culturally diverse groups. But it is going further. Wherever young people of different faiths meet and mingle and form friendships, love and marriage will inevitably follow in some cases. In the United States, where almost universal coeducation makes a very thorough job of the mixing process, it is now reported that about one third of all Catholics are marrying non-Catholics.

How do these marriages work out? The evidence we have so far gathered doesn't provide a very favorable picture.

Three separate American researches have sought to study the stability of the interfaith marriage. They all arrived at approximately the same result—namely, that the breakdown rate for marriages between people of different religions is between two and a quarter and two and a half times the rate for marriages where both partners are of the same faith. I would not myself accept this as a final verdict, because the researches in question suffered from certain limitations. But it represents the best information we have at present. It certainly offers no encouragement for the interfaith marriage.

Broken marriages are of course tragic, but they represent a comparatively small proportion of all marriages. What of the couples who, marrying across the frontiers of religious faith, stay together?

Many of them, we know, have a difficult time. Attitudes inculcated by religious training go deep, and in the close intimacy of marriage they have every opportunity to clash. In all marriages certain basic adjustments have to be made before a good relationship can be established. In a number of these areas the degree of potential tension is considerably increased by religious difference.

The in-laws, for example, nearly always begin by being opposed to such marriages. Occasionally the parents of one partner refuse to attend the wedding if it is celebrated in a church of an alien faith. The normal in-law adjustments which have to be made in every marriage can be greatly complicated by religious differences.

Again, all couples must face the task of social adjustment to the groups of friends and relatives with whom each was closely associated before marriage. Where husband and wife are of the same religion, these two groups often already know each other or at least have a basis for easy and natural acceptance of each other. But where their faiths differ, clashes may occur which result in marital tensions. To avoid trouble husband and wife may be forced to enjoy much of their social activity apart from each other.

Clashing loyalties arising from their religious practices can produce conflicts that never occur in a normal marriage. The wife wants to plan something at a particular time, only to find that her husband must then be present at some important function arranged by his church. The husband, at a time of financial pressure, is infuriated to find that his wife is giving to some religious cause money which he feels they can't really spare. Little incidents of this kind tend to arise frequently in the interfaith marriage. Conflicting views on political or municipal or social issues promulgated by their religious groups become the private arguments of the couple and easily develop into bitter quarrels.

Religious differences go deep into the personal life of the married couple. For instance, the issue of birth control, as viewed by the Catholic and non-Catholic partner in a mixed marriage, may have far-reaching implications for their sex relationship.

All these are, however, of secondary importance. Experience shows that far and away the major cause of tension in interfaith marriage is the upbringing and training of the children. To the young couple in love, parenthood seems a relatively remote experience. It is not easy for them to realize in advance the intensity of the conflicts that may be precipitated as the children come along.

The Roman Catholic Church anticipates this situation by requiring the non-Catholic partner to a mixed marriage to sign an agreement that the children will be brought up in the Catholic faith. Without this agreement the dispensation necessary to make the marriage valid in the eyes of the Roman Catholic Church cannot be granted, and for a devout Catholic, marriage without such dispensation can have serious consequences.

Confronted by this obstacle and seeing no way around it, the Protestant partner generally signs rather than abandon the idea of marriage. But when later the full implications of this undertaking are realized—it holds good even if the Catholic partner should die—a mood of rebellion may develop. This is particularly likely if by this time difficulties in adjustment have arisen in other areas of the marriage.

The action of the Roman Catholic Church in this regard has often been criticized. It seems to me that a church is quite entitled to make whatever rules it considers right for its members. It is not as if Catholics encourage interfaith marriage. In fact, they strongly *discourage* it.

In practice, however, the resulting difficulties are often acute. One of the deepest urges of parenthood is the wish to pass on to your offspring the values in life which you yourself cherish, and it can be a painful experience to watch your child assimilate convictions which are at variance with your own. I can recall the distress of a Protestant mother married to a devout Catholic, whose little boy came home from the parochial school and told her that he had learned that day that she would go to hell when she died.

It is difficult, in view of these facts, to see any argument in favor of interfaith marriages. In fact the leaders of all religious groups are of one mind in strongly discouraging such unions. One good reason that they do so is that all too often, exhausted by the tensions that lacerate their relationship, the couple give up their religious practices altogether in order to keep the peace. An American research found that this happened frequently in interfaith marriages. The result is that both partners are lost to religion, and their children are brought up without any spiritual training at all.

Despite the difficulties, however, it must not be thought that all couples of differing religious faith are unhappy. That is not so. I have encountered interfaith marriages which have seemingly been quite successful. I once tried, on the basis of personal interviews with fifty such couples, to discover what were the factors which seemed to promise the best results in such a marriage.

What emerged very clearly was that the successful marriages were generally those in which the couples had carefully and thoroughly faced and explored their differences beforehand. The couples who failed were those who with a vague optimism said, "We're in love, and that's all that matters. If we're going to have any problems, we'll face them when we come to them."

The wise couples who looked ahead tried to think through honestly the implications of their relationship. They faced and discussed the problems they thought lay ahead and agreed together on a policy to meet them. In some cases they made a careful study of each other's faith, through reading and sometimes through taking instruction. Though they retained their own religion (otherwise theirs would not have been interfaith marriages), they understood and respected each other's beliefs and convictions. On the basis of this understanding they were able to compose their differences as they arose.

Perhaps this is all just another way of saying that these were mature people. It is a characteristic of the mature that they think and plan ahead, leaving nothing to chance. Mature couples can overcome difficulties in marriage that for the less mature lead to disaster.

At one point, however, the testimony of these couples was significant. While their marriages were clearly successful, most of them were ready to admit that something was lacking. They loved each other and found marriage satisfying. Yet they were aware—especially in their most profound experiences of joy and of sorrow—that at the core of their relationship they could not be, as a couple of the same faith could be, completely of one heart and of one mind. The interfaith marriage cannot soar to the greatest heights of which marriage is capable.

The likelihood seems to be that interfaith marriages will go on increasing. We cannot prevent this by going back to the old attitudes of mutual suspicion and prejudice; that would be a reversal of human progress. I think we could, however, do something to lessen the misery and tragedy that these marriages often bring in their train.

What is needed is to study these marriages more closely and to make the facts about them more widely known. It seems, on the basis of our present information, that the outlook for this kind of marriage is not very good. If that is the case, this ought to be made known—together with the reasons—to young people in early adolescence. Too often parents, teachers, and religious leaders become concerned only when two young people of different faiths have already fallen deeply in love. To try to make them turn back then is like asking them to tear their hearts out, and they usually resist strongly.

If, however, through the religious organizations to which they belong, young people were plainly told the facts about interfaith marriage, they would be on their guard and would tend to avoid emotional involvements which they knew could not offer them the fullest happiness. The best chances for prevention seem to lie in this direction.

CHAPTER XVIII

WANDERING AFFECTIONS

Unfaithfulness in marriage can, as we have seen, introduce severe and even disastrous tensions into the relationship. There are many husbands and wives, however, who become emotionally involved in attachments that never lead to actual infidelity. Without any statistics to support me, I would venture the opinion that the majority of married people find themselves, at some time or another, beginning to fall in love with someone else. I think it is high time that we recognized this as a normal and natural, rather than an unhealthy and reprehensible, experience.

In this chapter we shall consider the problem created by this experience and the way in which the person concerned reacts to it. It is a problem which, like infidelity, may affect either husband or wife. When we discussed unfaithfulness, we treated the husband as the delinquent. In dealing with wandering affections let us consider that the wife is the person involved.

We have seen that the man Mary marries will probably be one of a number of men with whom her circumstances happen to throw her into close contact. Her decision may prove to be simple and clear-cut. It is just as likely that it may be agonizingly difficult, so that she is reduced almost to a state of nervous prostration as she struggles to choose between John and Arthur, both of whom want to marry her. In some respects John has what she wants. At other points Arthur seems a highly suitable match. The selection, for Mary, is not between black and white but between two closely similar shades of gray.

Many of us, in fact, spend the years of our youth falling

tumultuously and ecstatically in and out of love, experiencing the agony and the rapture of the great quest for a mate. We are sometimes in despair about our indecision and our capacity to change our minds.

Then at last we make the choice and marry. If we have chosen at all wisely, the joys and satisfactions that follow will leave us well content. We have played the field. Now we are ready to settle down to the serious business of establishing a lifelong relationship in its fullest possible depth and breadth.

"It is," as André Maurois has put it, "a formidable decision to make when one says: 'I bind myself for life; I have chosen; from now on my aim will be, not to search for someone who will please me, but to please the one I have chosen.'" We do this as a deliberate act of will, a dedication to a great and fundamental purpose—the founding of a new unit of human society, of a home and family.

Notice, however, that this doesn't mean that we have ceased to be able to love anyone else. The power to develop a new affection is still there. If Mary should have the misfortune to be widowed, her experience of loving and being loved is not necessarily over. Her need for love is indeed, just because she has had the experience, possibly greater for that reason. She may remarry and find great happiness in a second union. This, we are agreed, she can do without disloyalty to her former husband.

It is a logical implication of all this that Mary *could* fall in love again while still married to her husband and living with him. It is our traditional view that this is an act of disloyalty, and if we accept the principle of dedication to the task of marriage as Maurois has stated it, there is no doubt that this is the case.

However, let's be quite clear about this. There is no line of demarcation between the good people who don't find themselves falling in love again and the bad people who do. This false idea has been made a convenient excuse far too often for the breaking up of homes. "What could I do?" exclaims Daphne. "I was really in love with Gerald. So I couldn't help it, could I?" Daphne would probably be quite surprised, and possibly chastened, to learn that Margaret, paragon of wifely virtue that she is, once found herself nearly drawn into the whirlpool. The only real difference between the feeling she began to develop for Paul and the feeling Daphne developed for Gerald was that Margaret recognized it, sweet and exciting as it was, to be a wayward affection that she would not allow herself as a married woman to nourish. So she quietly stifled it, went through a period of dark dereliction, and found healing at last.

Margaret, of course, disclosed to no one the tumult that raged for a time within her breast. So neither Daphne nor anyone else ever knew about it. Perhaps that was a pity. Probably there are more who have shared Margaret's experience than most of us would ever imagine.

The conditions of our common life today throw men and women together in close and continuous associations. There are obvious gains in this new freedom but there are perils too. We rightly revile the iniquitous systems that kept wives under lock and key, allowing them out only under close escort or heavily veiled. But these elaborate systems were not established for nothing. And they were not only a safeguard against the predatory male. A woman's heart, it was well understood, could wander if she were given too much freedom.

Now the woman has almost unlimited freedom, and she knows that this is true. It was a woman, not a man, who recently gave it as her opinion that there is virtually no such thing as a platonic friendship between a man and woman of normal emotional endowment. The little god with his quiver of arrows is never far away, and he may with luck score a direct hit in the most unexpected of situations.

If this sounds like a plea for a return to Mid-Victorian customs, I am failing to make myself clear. We cannot go back— and I for one would not wish to do so if we could. What I am pleading for, however, is a realistic appraisal of the situation we have created for ourselves.

When Alice Jones, in the course of the job she does, has to spend eight hours a day in the same office with Peter Smith, this fact carries certain implications. It is possible that Mrs. Jones regards Mr. Smith as a pompous ass and that Mr. Smith considers Mrs. Jones a blundering idiot. The chances of emotional involvement are not in these circumstances great.

It is possible, however, that Alice may come to like and admire Peter and that Peter may for his part form the opinion that Alice is a very pleasant and attractive woman. This fact is likely to forge between them a bond of comradeship, out of which mutual understanding and responsive co-operation will probably grow. All this is advantageous for the smooth and efficient working of the office.

Suppose, however, that Peter is going through a period of disappointment in his marriage and that Alice has had to accept some emotional frustration in hers. There are unsatisfied needs in both of them which could very easily begin to grope toward each other along the channels of mutual respect and trust that have developed in their business association.

So one day Alice takes stock of the situation and becomes aware of the fact that she, of all people, is falling in love with another man. It has happened so imperceptibly that she is almost stunned by the realization. And she knows in her heart that she is confronted with a crisis.

This crisis is happening over and over again in our modern world. We have created the conditions that favor it. It can happen to anyone with a normal set of emotions.

No wrongdoing is necessarily involved in finding oneself in this situation. The pull of unexpected and unpredictable emotions can emerge in anyone's life. What constitutes the rights and wrongs of the situation is what one does about it when one becomes aware of what is happening.

What should Alice do? Some would simply say that if Peter appears to be a nicer and more desirable man than her husband, she should let events take their course. In that event there is no problem involved—at least, no problem of the kind we are discussing.

I am assuming, however, that Alice recognizes her loyalty to the bond which, forged by solemn vows, holds her to her marriage. Somehow, she is resolved, she must recover her balance and bring her wandering affections under control.

Ought she to break off all association with Peter, even if it means changing her job? A good deal depends on how far there has been any mutual acknowledgment between them of how they feel toward each other. If there hasn't been, Alice may be able to master her feelings, even though she continues to be with Peter most of the day. But this will not be easy.

If Alice is not sure that she can avoid being drawn deeper into the whirlpool of emotional involvement, it is much the best policy to get right out of danger. Even if she thinks she can handle her feelings, but isn't sure, it is probably better not to expose herself to the risk of failing to do so.

If she and Peter have mutually acknowledged the attraction they feel toward each other, it is highly unlikely that they can go back to the more formal type of relationship they knew before this happened. The further they have gone, the greater the difficulty will be. Where love has been mutually declared and it has become clear to one or both that the association must be renounced, it is tempting Providence to continue to meet each other. The only sensible course is to make a complete and final break.

This is always painful. The further the relationship has been allowed to develop, the sharper will be the pain. The break is usually followed by a season of utter misery and heartache. But if the resolution to finish has been wholehearted and sincere, a slow process of healing soon begins. Alice comes to realize that the meaning of life for her is wider than any single relationship. The realization that she has retained her integrity fortifies her spirit.

In time the struggle is over, and the cloud has passed. She is able to turn again to her marriage with some sense of purpose and to build again the walls that had begun to crumble. When the situation is wisely handled, a little tongue of bright flame reappears and kindles again the love that was thought to be dead.

If her husband has been unaware of what was happening, ought Alice to tell him? There can be no general answer to this question. I would suggest that the best way for Alice to answer it would be to tell someone else first—some trusted, mature, neutral person with whom she can discuss her predicament frankly and freely. In this discussion she should ask herself honestly whether she is wholeheartedly *willing* to tell her husband if she decides that it is the right thing to do so.

If she is willing, then she is free to concentrate her attention upon whether it is the kindest thing for her husband, and the best course in the future interest of her marriage, to tell him.

Marriage, as Maurois wisely reminds us, involves a choice, and the choice we make involves a commitment. We cannot be sure that we are making the wisest of all possible choices. The probability is that we are not. As we move on through life, other possibilities will appear to us, new emotions will stir within us. We are human, and it must be so. But being human also involves us in responsibilities and loyalties. There is much truth in the saying of Emil Brunner that marriage is based not so much on love as on fidelity. I would prefer to say that love is not love unless fidelity is its heart's core.

CHAPTER XIX

CHILDLESSNESS

"It's such a disappointment to us," said Frances. "We've been married four years now. We agreed that I'd keep on my job for the first two years, so we didn't want to start a family then. But after that, we expected a baby quite soon.

"After a year of trying, we both got pretty depressed. I felt all on edge. Every month I'd keep hoping—then my hopes would be dashed again. John was very understanding at first. But in time he got snappy too. You see, he also wants children very much. He doesn't say a lot, but I get the feeling that he thinks I'm a failure. I suppose he's right. A woman who can't produce children has always been considered a sort of second-rate wife.

"John keeps pestering me to talk to our doctor about it. Somehow I'm scared to do so. I'm afraid he'll tell me I can't ever have children. I just don't know how John would take that. It might be the end of our marriage."

Few experiences can be more poignant than the awareness, breaking upon a wife with strong maternal instincts, that childlessness may be her portion. As the months go by, hope deferred makes her sick at heart. She meets her former girl friends, who proudly display their offspring. She sees her neighbors pushing their strollers past her gate. She reads with exasperation of young girls, and older married women, having babies they don't want. "Why does this have to happen to me?" she cries. "Why? Why? Why?"

This is not merely a woman's private problem. It can soon become a marriage problem. Nothing cements the unity of man and wife like the solemn wonder of that exalted moment when they stand together, hand in hand, looking down upon their sleeping child. Love is creative, and its supreme act of creation is the coming of a new life. An unfruitful marriage has hazards all its own. It is significant that couples without children divorce each other at a decidedly higher rate than those who have families.

Added to the wife's personal frustration and her sense of having failed her husband is the fact that society has always tended to look askance at the "barren" woman. In many civilizations the woman's main function is to bear children. If she fails here, she is good for little else. It is as if a curse rested upon her. The desperate lengths to which the childless wife in a primitive society is willing to go, in submitting herself to the humiliating and fantastic rituals required by black magic, is the external evidence of her inner desperation.

The modern wife, fortunately, is valued for herself, whether she has children or not. She need not cry with Rachel, "Give me children, or I die." Yet she cannot wholly escape some participation in Rachel's anguish, as the accusing voices within and without whisper to her that she is a failure.

What can we say to Frances and to the nearly fifteen per cent of all wives who share her problem?

We can in fact say a great deal. Our understanding of the causes of childlessness has greatly increased in recent years. Indeed, there is hardly any field of medical research where more progress has been made and still is being made. There are certain facts which every married couple, and indeed every adult, should know.

First, it should be clearly stated that the causes of childlessness are now known to be about equally distributed between husbands and wives. Yet human history is full of stories of men who rejected their wives because they were "barren." In many of these cases it was just as likely to have been the men themselves whose fertility was deficient.

Victor pestered Cynthia to "go and have an operation or something" when, after six years of marriage, she had failed to bear him a son and heir. Finally she went to her doctor. A thorough investigation found no apparent defect in her, and Victor was asked to go for an examination. After many protests he finally went—to learn that he was incurably sterile, the result of untreated gonorrhea contracted from a prostitute when he was eighteen. He was so humiliated that he would not allow the doctor to tell Cynthia the true facts.

Second, everyone should know that some (though not all) of the causes of childlessness can now be cured. Quite high percentages have been given to indicate the chances of cure, but it is doubtful how reliable they are. What is certain, however, is that any couple who have been trying intelligently to start a family for a year, without success, should not hesitate to seek medical aid.

I said "trying intelligently." There is no sense in bothering busy doctors unnecessarily. The important point for couples seeking a pregnancy is to know that intercourse should take place at the right time. If the wife keeps a six months' record of the dates on which her periods begin, she should be able easily to calculate the range of possible dates on which the next may be expected. A similar range of dates fourteen days earlier will represent her fertile period. This time, including a couple of days before and after, represents the time within which the sex relations of the couple should be concentrated.

If this doesn't have the desired effect, the time has come for medical help to be sought. The general practitioner usually lacks the resources to carry through a thorough investigation. Too often in the past the family doctor has been content to give the wife a routine examination and leave it at that. Frances should definitely not be satisfied to leave it at that. She should insist on being referred to a specialist or clinic with facilities for the comprehensive examination of both husband and wife.

Married couples are often reticent about making the necessary move, and put it off. There is no need to do this. The doctors who give these tests fully understand how men and women feel about them and go out of their way to put their patients at their ease. None of the routine tests involves any pain. Nor should they cause any embarrassment.

In the case of the husband, the matter is extremely simple. All that is necessary is for him to deliver to the doctor, in a sterile container provided for the purpose, a specimen of seminal fluid as recent as possible. This is then carefully examined under a microscope. First, it is necessary to discover whether any sperms (the male seeds that cause the wife to conceive) are present at all.

It should be clearly understood that a man may be sexually quite normal and yet not be producing a single sperm. Many people confuse potency and fertility. They would seem to be related—in fact, they are not. A highly-sexed man may be totally incapable of producing a child, while a man with a very weak sex drive may be highly fertile.

If no sperms are found, there is obviously no point in going further with tests for the wife. However, sperms may be present, but in insufficient numbers—hundreds of millions are normally produced in order to give one a chance of getting through. Or the sperms may not have the vitality to keep swimming long enough to reach their goal. They may even not be properly formed, so that they swim round in circles and make no progress.

All these points can be checked in the microscopic examination. If something is found to be wrong, there is no need to give up hope. Quite possibly there is a remedy. Further tests on the husband will then be necessary.

The routine examination of the wife will include a test to see whether her natural secretions are overacid. This would lead to the destruction of the sperms in large numbers, because acid kills them. This difficulty can sometimes be overcome simply by using an alkaline douche before intercourse.

The doctor will also want to test whether the Fallopian tubes, along which the egg cells or "ova" travel to the womb, are clear. Sometimes they are blocked, and this is why the woman fails to conceive. Gently pumping a harmless gas into the womb and watching to see whether the pressure gradually falls will soon show whether the pathway is open or closed.

Other kinds of tests may be needed. But this brief description should be enough to show that there are many possible reasons why that baby doesn't come along and that it is obviously more sensible for Frances to get to know the facts than to eat her heart out in secret sorrow.

The chances are that the medical investigation will open up possibilities of a cure. If not, at least John and Frances will know where they stand.

If there is no hope that they may expect a child of their own, there are three possibilities open to them.

The first is adoption. Many childless couples have found deep and lasting fulfillment in taking into their homes a little child who might otherwise have lacked the love and care they were able to offer. Adoption has become so acceptable today that the demand is very heavy, and the adoption societies have long waiting lists. But if a couple decide to have a child of their own, they have to wait till conception takes place, and then another nine months after that. So waiting is part of the process either way!

The second possibility is artificial insemination by an anonymous donor. This is a comparatively new procedure, hedged about with ethical and legal uncertainties and condemned by some religious bodies. Nevertheless, it seems to have met the needs of at least some couples who do not object to it on ethical grounds and who have met the rather rigorous conditions which the doctor usually requires.

Finally, a couple may decide simply to accept their childlessness and to try to compensate for it in other ways. So long as they face the facts realistically, this should be quite possible. A childless marriage involves certain hazards of its own, but that doesn't imply that it cannot be happy. Creative love can and should find expression in other ways than in parenthood. How effectively this can be achieved will depend upon the resourcefulness of the individual couple. But it certainly can be done. Some childless marriages have turned out to be supremely happy ones.

CHAPTER XX

DRIFTING APART

When married people tell me their love has died, I sometimes think it might be more accurate to say that they have killed it. I am not thinking of violent, brutal acts of dark betrayal. I just mean that the flame of love has gradually waned and guttered out from sheer neglect.

Any fool, it has been said, can fall in love. But to *keep* in love—that is another matter. One of the great illusions of our time is that love is self-sustaining. It is not. Love must be fed and nurtured, constantly renewed. That demands ingenuity and consideration, but first and foremost, it demands *time*.

Consider George and Elaine. Before their marriage they spent long, leisurely hours together, away from the throb and roar of daily life. They planned trips to pleasant, exciting places, and of course they insisted on going alone. There wasn't anything unusual about that. All courting couples do the same.

When it came to saying "Good night," they felt the sharp pain of parting. Then they would sigh wistfully and say, "But soon we'll be married, and then we'll be together all the time. How wonderful that will be!"

It *was* wonderful on the honeymoon. Everything went well. But after they got back, somehow the dream didn't come true. George was away all day at work, and so was Elaine at first. By the time they got home they were tired, and there was so much to attend to—supper to prepare, the clearing up to do, odd jobs to finish. Sometimes George had to go out again as soon as the meal was over, and he wasn't home till late. Elaine had choir practice one night, a course she was taking on another, some other engagement on a third. The free nights just never seemed to be free. There would be housework or office work to catch up with, or someone would drop in and talk. At the week ends there was visiting their families, or letters to write, or work to do in the house or garden. It was all necessary, and a lot of it quite pleasant, but somehow it wasn't what they had dreamed about. Gone were the long, carefree hours together when they could just talk and enjoy each other.

When the children arrived it was worse than ever. Elaine could never pin down just what took so much of the time. All she knew was that the time went—all of it. And George became more and more busy. Of course it was encouraging that they were putting him on so many important committees. But it meant his being out night after night, and by the week end he was too tired to do much. And now, when they sat down to talk, it was always a sort of business meeting to decide what to do about Johnnie's school report, or how to arrange their schedules so that they could both have the car when they wanted it next Saturday, or whether it would be best to have the vacuum cleaner repaired or face the cost of a new one. The long, deep talks in which they opened their hearts to each other were now only a wistful memory, and even when they made love, they either had an ear alerted for the strident summons of the telephone or doorbell, or an eye on the clock and the feeling that they must hurry and get to sleep or they'd never be up in time in the morning.

What happened to George and Elaine is what happens, in one way or another, to most married couples. I recall a successful professional man, greatly in demand, describing his heavy schedule. Someone asked him when he saw his wife. With a wan smile he replied, "We pass on the stairs now and then." I know a young businessman so absorbed in making money that his wife might almost as well be a widow with a generous pension. I know another man whose wife is much engaged in public work, who said to me recently, "If I want to talk to her alone, I have to make an appointment a week ahead."

So we jest. These things have to be, we say, shrugging our shoulders. But is that true?

I don't believe it. Almost every couple could, if they really made up their minds about it, take time to sustain their love. They are defeated not by an inexorable fate, but by their own bad planning, false values, and lack of imagination.

Oddly enough, George and Elaine were organizing their lives well in nearly every other area. They took care to avoid waste or misuse of their money. They had an agreed policy about work and responsibility in the running of the home. Only in the planning of the time they owed to each other were they slapdash and disorganized. They tried hard to be fair to everyone—except themselves.

I asked them why. The first reason they gave was interesting. Both acknowledged a feeling that they shouldn't need much time alone together, because as a married couple they should have outgrown that kind of thing. "It's natural enough," said Elaine, "that courting couples should want to be alone. But when two married people want to break away from the group and go off by themselves, it seems odd. Isn't there something slightly comic about a husband and wife who want to sit and hold hands in the park?"

Maybe that's why married couples often put their plans to do something together a long way down on the list of priorities. If Elaine wants George to take her out in the car to see the sunset and George has a business letter to write, it's usually the letter that gets attended to. If George suggests going to bed early to make love and Elaine has a pile of ironing to finish, the ironing often wins. "Get everything else done first, and then what's left is ours" seems to be the usual guiding principle. And of course what's left all too often is no time at all. Love, which once came first, now comes last. Is it any wonder that it languishes under such treatment?

Another reason that came up was that married people always reckon they can fulfill their personal plans "some other time." George is asked to help to run the Boy Scout display on the night he and Elaine had planned to go to the theater. "I suppose I ought to," says George; "it only happens once a year." "All right dear," sighs Elaine. "Maybe it *would* be selfish to put our own enjoyment first. We can go to the theater some other night instead." But the other night usually never comes.

Sometimes it's the children who block the way. I know a couple who wouldn't go out together because the wife felt that *their* children were far too precious to be left with a baby sitter. This exaggerated sense of duty led to trouble. The husband, after a few dreary evenings out by himself, began surreptitiously to seek elsewhere the female company which his wife ought to have provided.

The idea that time alone together is a sort of selfish indulgence which high-minded married couples don't need is a dangerous fallacy. The truth is that love, in marriage or out of it, continues to be fresh, vigorous, and sparkling only if we keep it properly nurtured.

Life in these days provides unprecedented opportunities to do this. Spacious leisure is ours which our forefathers never knew. Yet in our folly we have cluttered it all up with a whirl of activities and a plethora of supposed obligations which simply will not bear critical investigation in the light of the sacrifices we are making to fulfill them. Of what real value is all the new spare time which our technological age is making possible for us, if we do not use it to cultivate the great arts of living and of loving? What will it profit us to be prosperous, to live in a fine house and eat the best food, if we are starved of love? Any psychiatrist will tell you that at least half his patients are love-starved people, and one of the reasons is that either they or their parents, deluded by a false sense of values, have not taken time to generate the warmth and tenderness which a glowing, vital, love relationship imparts to the human personality.

The greatest tragedy of all is when married people, having failed to cultivate their love life with each other, turn elsewhere to fill the gnawing emptiness in their hearts. Many a frustrated husband, guiltily taking another woman to some secluded place, might have found it just as exciting to be taking the wife he thinks he no longer cares for, dressed in her best and in gay, carefree mood. The irony of it is that he never sees his wife like that any more. They meet only amid the stress and turmoil of life, where they have come to symbolize for each other the dull, drab routines from which they long to escape. The idea that they might escape together, and re-create their love in the process, has not occurred to them.

I know a married couple who resolved that, as a duty to themselves and each other, they would go away together for four long week ends each year. They were resolute enough to book the dates well ahead, and they burned their bridges by paying for their hotel reservations in advance. When the time came, there were all kinds of reasons against their going. Once they were so out of tune with each other that the plan nearly broke down. But always, when once they were away and relaxed, the experience brought a deep and satisfying renewal of their love.

Almost any couple could do that. The affluent, no doubt, will want to fly to Paris. But the same purpose can be served on a modest budget with a little imagination. You couldn't afford it? Are you sure? Plenty of people who rank themselves poor spend much more on drinks, cigarettes, and patent medicines in the attempt to steady their throbbing nerves, and all these are much poorer palliatives for the tensions of modern life. What about the children? Where there's a will, there's a way. I know a group of couples who relieve each other by taking in each other's families for occasional week ends, and it works very well.

If every couple stuck out for four long week ends away together each year, there might be a good deal more contentment and less friction in our homes. But I wouldn't be making my point if I suggested that the only way to run a home successfully is to keep running away from it. The art of taking time to sustain love must be practiced primarily in the home itself.

I can't tell you in detail how to do this. The recipe will vary from couple to couple. In each case the method must be worked out to meet the objective—which is to recapture the relaxed, cozy intimacy which every couple once knew when, as lovers, they just enjoyed each other and let the world go by. This experience, far from wasting time, is a vital source of that pulsing zest for life which so many crave with increasing hopelessness as the years pass. The clue to contented living is to love and to be loved. It is as simple as that.

There is a subtle vanity in many of us which makes us persuade ourselves that we can do without the simple, elementary necessities. Some think they can work all the time and never stop for rest and relaxation. Some believe they can dwell entirely on a material plane and ignore spiritual values. And some delude themselves that they can make marriage work and run a home, while they let love perish for sheer neglect. In each case such folly only brings down in the end those who practice it. There are laws of our being which we challenge only to destroy ourselves, our hopes, and our dreams.

I suggest that all married people who read this should pause and ask themselves a few simple questions. Are you taking time to keep in love? Are you sustaining in each other the warm, tender affection which flows between all true lovers? Do you find yourselves periodically refreshed and renewed by the mutual delights of body, mind, and spirit which you share? Are there tensions in life which you cannot bear because you are foolishly denying yourselves the healing and comfort which husband and wife should draw from their unity and fellowship?

If you have to acknowledge that you have been neglectful of the frail but fragrant flower of love, I would ask you to remember that your time is, after all, your life. As the moments tick by, and the sand runs swiftly through the hourglass, it is life itself that is slowly slipping away. You take time to work and time to play, time to eat and time to sleep, time for personal interests and time for social responsibilities. Surely, surely in all this wealth of time which is yours, you can take time to keep in love.

TO THOSE IN TROUBLE

It is a disturbing experience for men and women who went into marriage with eager expectations and high hopes to become aware that all is not going well. You put so much of yourself into marriage—your hopes of future happiness, your dreams of the children who would take up the torch of life from you and carry it into the future, your need for close and comforting companionship, and so much else. To see all this slipping from your grasp, to find resentment in your heart where once there was warm, outgoing love, to know only bitterness and heartache instead of tenderness and affection—this is indeed to feel that your world is crumbling into ruins.

Throughout the years thousands of husbands and wives who have been undergoing this tragic experience have turned to me for help. I have not always been able to do for them all I could have wished. But I have tried to be understanding, and sometimes together we have found a happy way out. I pause now, as I write, to think of one couple after another for whom the shadow passed and who are now again living in the sunshine.

I want, first, to offer you hope. I have learned in my work as a marriage counselor never to despair. There is always a way out. No problem is insoluble. The resources of the human spirit to meet and to triumph over adversity have amazed me again and again. There seems to be almost nothing that men and women cannot do when they are wholly resolved upon it. In marriage the will to succeed is of vital importance. I have known situations that seemed altogether hopeless, yet somehow in the end the problems were resolved. I have known other marriages in which there was really very little wrong but which failed because husband and wife lacked the determination to make them work. So first, I want to offer you hope.

Second, I would like to give you perspective. People under emotional stress find it very hard to see straight. They get the situation out of focus, look at the very worst side of each other, and can easily misjudge the possibilities of recovery. They become desperately tired of all the struggling and striving, the conflict and tension. All they want is somehow to get away from it all, to escape into peace.

In this mood people can do foolish things. I have known husbands and wives who started divorce proceedings just because they were too exhausted to think of anything else to do. Then they found themselves moving relentlessly toward what had looked like a way out but wasn't really a way out at all. Some people, no doubt, solve their problems by getting a divorce. Others only find, when it is all over, that they have escaped into an abyss of loneliness and heartache. Divorce can lead, also, to tremendous complications for the children of a marriage.

Third, I want to offer you practical help. When marital conflict reaches a certain point, the couple themselves become incapable of coping with it. They are emotionally too deeply involved. Every time they try to have a calm discussion it flares up into a bitter argument.

What this means is that they need an outside mediator. The lines of communication between them are so tangled up that only someone detached from the situation is able to see how the confusion can be cleared.

This raises a difficulty for many people. We are brought up in a proud tradition of self-sufficiency and independence. We are taught that we should cope with our own troubles and solve our own problems. To ask outside help in our personal affairs seems somehow humiliating, a sign of weakness.

It *is* good for us to stand on our own feet and solve our own problems—*if we can.* But a point may come for any one of us at which the problem is really beyond us. It has got us beaten, and we know it.

At this point it is no longer virtuous to refuse stubbornly to ask for help. It becomes a sign of weakness and not of strength, of foolishness and not of intelligence. We don't admire the man who dies because he refuses to call a doctor or who ruins his car because he goes on tinkering with it when he doesn't really know what he's doing.

So a point comes in marriage problems when the logical, sensible, mature, intelligent thing to do is to recognize that someone who is completely outside the situation can cope with it better than you can.

Many people come to recognize this in the end. Some of them unburden themselves to relatives and friends. This can be very helpful in some cases. In others, unfortunately, it doesn't help at all. Relatives and friends are not as a rule unbiased. They tend to take sides. Or they give advice. More and more we are coming to see the inadequacy of advice-giving. One person simply cannot live another's life for him.

A better way is to take your problem to your doctor or to a minister of religion. Often, however, these professional people are very busy. Sometimes, too, they have not been trained to deal with marriage problems and are themselves the first to acknowledge their inadequacy.

The best way of all is to take the problem to a marriage counselor. I have stressed this again and again throughout the book. These counselors, if they are properly accredited, are mature, understanding, and completely trustworthy. They have been trained to understand the causes of marriage failure. I know many of them personally, and I can assure you that they are very fine people.

How do you get in touch with a marriage counselor? Don't rely on your telephone directory, less still on people who advertise their services. Unfortunately there are a few "quacks" in this field.

Make inquiries through your minister or physician. If they can't refer you to a marriage counselor, try any reputable social service agency in your district (especially a Family Service organization), or the psychology or sociology department of any nearby university or college. Failing all these sources, try some of the national organizations listed at the end of this book.

Once you have located a competent marriage counselor, telephone for an appointment. When the time comes to go along, you need feel no apprehension. The counselor knows how you feel and is eager to put you at your ease. Remember, his sole object as a marriage counselor is to help men and women toward success in their marriage.

When you see the counselor, what will happen? He (or she) will ask you to explain just what has happened. You will be encouraged to say just what you feel about it all, while the counselor listens sympathetically and asks an occasional question. The foundation of a counselor's training is to make him a patient, sympathetic listener, because we know that this is first and foremost what people in marriage difficulties need.

The counselor will not judge you. Whatever you have done, you will be fully accepted. You will not be put "on the spot" or made to feel uncomfortable. That would achieve nothing. You will not be asked to talk about anything you don't wish to discuss, and there will be no embarrassing probing into your private affairs. On the other hand, you are free to discuss the most intimate matters if it will help you to do so. The decision rests with you. And of course everything you say will be treated in the strictest confidence. This is quite fundamental to the whole work of marriage counseling. The counselor will not, for instance, disclose to your marriage partner anything you want kept private.

In this atmosphere of freedom and privacy you will find that you are able to look at your marriage problems in a new way. The counselor will help you to see just what has gone wrong and why. It isn't a question of deciding who is at fault. A counselor refuses to act as a judge. All that matters is that two people are in difficulty, and they need to discover what is the best course of action to help them out of their misery and distress. The counselor will not decide the course of action for them. It isn't his job to give people advice. He will work with them patiently, encouraging them to find the best solution themselves.

Obviously this can't always be done in one interview. Marriage problems are often quite complicated, and it's amazing how much there is to tell and how quickly an hour passes. So be prepared if necessary to go back for another interview or even for several more. The counselor isn't a magician. Your problem probably took a long time to develop, and it's only reasonable that it should take time to solve.

To do the job properly, the counselor should see both husband and wife. Almost always they are interviewed separately, because they feel freer to talk about the problem when they are alone. The counselor will do his best to help you even if your partner can't or won't come. But obviously he has a much better chance if he can work with both husband and wife.

It is always best to take a marriage problem to a counselor before it has become very serious. Many people adopt the attitude that they should try everything else first, and then, if all else fails, they can call in the marriage counselor. This is a mistaken attitude, because while less experienced people are tinkering with the problem, valuable time is being lost and the situation may be deteriorating rapidly. The right time to seek marriage counseling is *immediately when the couple become aware that they have a problem which they seem unable to solve by themselves.*

One thing you can be quite sure about. No marriage counselor will ever tell you that your problem is too trivial and that you are wasting his time. He knows from his training that large and serious problems grow out of small beginnings, and every counselor believes fervently that prevention is better than cure.

What will it cost to get this help? The fees of counselors vary. You should not hesitate to ask, when making an appointment or at the first interview, what will be involved financially. Tell the counselor exactly what your circumstances are.

More and more people nowadays are turning to the marriage counselor for help in their trouble. I have explained in detail just what this involves, because I want you to see how reasonable and sensible it is. There will always be a certain number of marriages that fail. This the marriage counselor fully recognizes. He does not expect to be able to save every marriage that is brought to him. If the couple decide that they can't go on together, he accepts their decision. What he is concerned about is that every reasonable possibility of making the marriage work should be explored.

Surely you would agree. To end a marriage if there is any hope of making it work is a needless tragedy for all concerned. There is sometimes a quite simple solution, but the couple themselves, strained and tense, are unable to see it. Taking their problem to a counselor and working at it sincerely with his help provides a real opportunity to find that solution if it exists.

In this book I have tried to discuss many of the difficulties that arise in marriage. I may have touched on your problem, or I may have missed it. If I have touched on it, I may have given you some clues toward finding your own solution. But if not, I urge you to seek counseling help. Reading about marriage difficulties can be helpful in many cases. Of that I am sure. But in other cases the only help that is really effective comes through talking it out with someone who can apply his knowledge and experience, not in a general way, but to the particular, unique circumstances of an individual marriage.

FOR FURTHER READING

There are many books on marriage. Rather than give a long list, I am confining this bibliography to ten volumes. I have chosen them because they are easy to read and because they are recently published books or recent revisions of old books. Most of them contain bibliographies in which many other books on marriage and family living are listed.

Blood, Robert O. *Marriage.* New York: Free Press of Glencoe, 1962.

Bowman, Henry A. *Marriage for Moderns.* New York: McGraw-Hill Book Co., 1954.

Butterfield, Oliver M. *Sex Life in Marriage.* Chicago: Emerson Books, 1947.

Christensen, Harold T. *Marriage Analysis.* New York: Ronald Press Co., 1950.

Davis, Maxine. *The Sexual Responsibility of Women.* New York: Dial Press, 1956.

Duvall, Evelyn M., and Hill, Reuben. *When You Marry.* New York: Association Press, 1953.

Landis, Judson T. and Mary G. *Building a Successful Marriage.* Englewood Cliffs, N. J.: Prentice-Hall, 1953.

Magoun, F. Alexander. *Love and Marriage.* New York: Harper & Brothers, 1956.

Peterson, James A. *Toward a Successful Marriage.* New York: Charles Scribner's Sons, 1960.

Stone, Abraham and Hannah. *A Marriage Manual.* New York: Simon & Schuster, 1952.

ORGANIZATIONS

Here is a list of national organizations from which information about marriage counseling services in the United States can be obtained:

American Association of Marriage Counselors, 27 Woodcliff Dr., Madison, New Jersey.

American Institute of Family Relations, 5287 Sunset Blvd., Los Angeles 27, California.

Central Conference of American Rabbis (Committee on Marriage, Family, and the Home), 40 West 68th Street, New York 23, N.Y.

Family Service Association of America, 44 East 23rd St., New York, N.Y.

National Association for Mental Health, 10 Columbus Circle, New York 19, N.Y.

National Catholic Welfare Conference (Family Life Bureau), 1312 Massachusetts Ave., N.W., Washington 5, D.C.

National Council of the Churches of Christ in the U.S.A. (Department of Family Life), 475 Riverside Dr., New York, N.Y.

National Council on Family Relations, 1219 University Ave., S.E., Minneapolis 14, Minnesota

Planned Parenthood Federation of America, 501 Madison Ave., New York 22, N.Y.

INDEX

155